Room at the Inn:

Guide to Historic B&Bs, Hotels and Country Inns
Close to the Twin Cities

Laura Zahn

Down to Earth Publications
St. Paul, Minnesota

Laura Zahn is a St. Paul, Minn., writer and public relations consultant who specializes in travel. Her work has been published in many newspapers and magazines, including the Chicago Sun-Times, Dallas Morning News, Detroit News, Hartford Courant, Kansas City Star, Mpls.-St. Paul Magazine, Minneapolis Star and Tribune and St. Paul Pioneer Press-Dispatch. Zahn has worked in public relations in Minnesota and as a reporter and editor on newspapers in Alaska and Minnesota.

Published by **Down to Earth Publications**
        873 Lincoln
        St. Paul, MN 55105

First printing, October 1986.

Library of Congress Cataloging in Publication Data.
Zahn, Laura Claire
        Room at the Inn:
        Guide to Historic B&Bs, Hotels and Country Inns
        Close to the Twin Cities
1. Bed and Breakfast Accommodations - Middle West - Directories
TX 907.   86-50888

ISBN 0-939301-00-8 (softcover)

Map by Jim Miller

Photos by Laura Zahn, except:
        P. 97, courtesy of the DeSoto House Hotel
        P. 117, sketch of Kettle Falls Hotel by Ron Schmidt, courtesy of
        Voyageurs National Park

Cover art provided by Mrs. B's Historic Lanesboro Inn, Old Rittenhouse Inn, the Archer House and Canterbury Inn B&B

Printing by Viking Press, Eden Prairie, Minnesota

To Jim,
with whom I would like to stay
in these places...

Many people were helpful in making this book more than an idea.

Special thanks to Ann Barkelew, Burt Cohen, Maxine Jeffris, Marcia Kelly, Toyse Kyle, Jim Miller, Jan Nelson, Kathy O'Neill, Pam Thorsen, Mary Ziegenhagen and some new friends in special places.

Table of Contents

Please Note: Driving times from the Twin Cities Metro Area may vary depending on starting point, speed and road conditions.

INTRODUCTION
What to Know About Using This Guide

For a very long time, it seemed that "getting away from it all" for many Minnesotans meant a week in the summer at the family cabin or at a resort housekeeping cottage.

But we have changed.

Fewer people are waiting until retirement to enjoy life. Many two-career couples are so busy they rarely see each other. More parents feel less guilty for making arrangements to leave the kids at home and getting away *from* them, instead of *with* them.

We want to get away more often, for shorter periods of time, and stay closer to home.

And we want to treat ourselves. We don't seem to want super-slick city hotels or the stimulation of blaring TVs or ringing phones on these getaways. Instead, we're looking toward lodging in facilities that are warm and personal - even down to the decorating, the homey feeling often inspired by early American decor and Victorian antiques. We want to return to a slower pace, if only for overnight. And we may want to rekindle some romance in a four-poster bed or a double whirlpool.

This book is intended as a guide for Twin Cities residents to those getaways. It provides more information than is available in any other single publication.

What is a B&B, anyway?

B&B stands for **Bed and Breakfast**. For years, travelers to Europe have enjoyed inexpensive accommodations in the extra bedroom of a local family. They found that B&Bs also were a good way to meet friendly local people.

The B&B movement is catching on in America. In the Twin Cities area, historic B&Bs are not necessarily economical, but they remain a good way to meet our neighbors. And they are much different than a motel or hotel.

A rough definition of a B&B might be: A home, lived in by the owner or manager, which has one or more guest rooms for rent overnight, which often share bathrooms and other common rooms, such as living and dining rooms, and which have some kind of breakfast available before check-out the next day included as part of the overnight rate.

From there, it's impossible to draw a picture of a typical historic B&B. But, in general, most B&Bs are cozy and homey. Guests are, afterall, sharing someone's home, which more than one B&B owner/operater said she believes is a privilege and should be treated as such. Meeting your hosts is part of the personalized service, as is perhaps eating in their kitchen on their china, or sitting by the fire in their parlor.

Do not expect phones or TVs in the rooms, free shower caps or shoe-shine cloths, and don't call for reservations at midnight. Be as courteous as you would if you were to be a houseguest in a friend's home, and don't hesitate to ask for whatever would make you comfortable (after all, you're paying for it).

While some B&Bs welcome children, others are designed as weekend or special event adult getaways and not set up for children of any age who may disturb other guests. If it's not clear, ask the owner.

Other rough definitions to help explain how this guide is organized:

Hotel: A major lodging facility with possibly several dozen rooms, restaurants, bars and off-street parking in its own lot, with services such as round-the-clock desk clerks and personnel to carry bags, bring room service, turn down the bed, bring an extra towel and clean the rooms; with amenities such as TVs and phones.

Hotels are more impersonal and, therefore, much more private than B&Bs.

Country Inn: Basically, a cross between a B&B and a hotel. A country inn typically has some of the more personal atmosphere of a B&B with much of the privacy of a hotel. Rooms usually are in the same structure (most often, upstairs) as the lobby and dining areas.

Country inns may have more rooms available than a B&B, but possibly still less than 10. Sometimes they are made from a former home or mansion, or from a former hotel. The owner may check in the guests and remember their names. Like in a hotel, TVs and phones in each room are more likely than in a B&B, and breakfast usually is not included in the room rate.

And, finally, the definition used for **Historic:** The lodging structure must have been more than 50 years old and, hopefully, of some historic significance to the local area. Several of the structures included in this guide are listed on the National Register of Historic Places.

Who is included in the book?

The historic B&Bs, hotels and country inns listed in this guide are either fairly well known in the Twin Cities area or they should be. Doubtless a few were left out through no fault of their own, but because they were not known to the author.

Only independent B&Bs, inns and hotels were included which may be reserved by individuals (as opposed to through an association or reservation service).

No facility paid to be included in this book.

All facilities were personally visited, except the Kettle Falls Hotel (closed until 1988) and some of the Galena Guest Houses (pp. 100-101). This does not, however, count as an endorsement of any facility or as any kind of "inspection." Rather, this book was intended as a guide to provide specific information in one publication.

The establishments written about vary widely in what they offer guests in rooms, services, rates, meals and general atmosphere. Their cleanliness or any other aspect of service may vary. Information was provided in an attempt to paint a realistic picture of what each establishment is like; readers must draw their own conclusions about whether they would like to stay there, based on personal tastes and preferences. For example, the type of decor described simply may not suit you. No place is for everyone; B&Bs aren't for everyone, either.

Who is not included?

Some historic structures were left out because they did not seem to fit the concept of types of facilities for which this guide was intended.

Some were left out because, frankly, they did not seem to be the type of place the audience of this book would want to visit.

Also, some structures were left out because they did not feel historic inside and out. For example, a facility was not included if the building itself was historic, but no attempt was made to carry the historic theme through to the interior decor to capture the feeling of staying in an historic structure. Conversely, if the interior was done in, say, Early American, but the building was modern, it also was not included.

Resorts and wilderness lodges are not included, though there are many fine, historic facilities available.

A Note about Licensing

Licensing requirements vary from B&Bs to hotels to country inns, and from state to state. Those B&Bs which are members of the Minnesota Historic B&B Association are licensed by the state of Minnesota as a criterion of membership. If you have concerns about whether a facility is licensed, ask the owner/operator or contact the state Department of Health or the county health department in which the facility is located.

The Minnesota Historic B&B Association

This association was formed in 1983 as a support group for proprietors of historic B&Bs. Criteria for membership include a building that is more than 50 years old and historic in nature, and licensing by the state for food handling and overnight accommodations.

In addition to offering information, education and services, the members often recommend each other or refer guests to other member B&Bs which have openings. Eventually, president Pam Thorsen hopes the group will have one phone number through which guests can reserve a room at any of the member B&Bs.

Members included in this book are: Bluff Creek Inn, Canterbury Inn B&B, Christopher Inn, The Cosgrove, Country B&B, Driscoll's for Guests, Historic Taylors Falls Jail, The Lowell House, The Mansion, Mrs. B's Historic Lanesboro Inn, Pratt-Taber Inn, The Rahilly House, The Rivertown Inn, Thorwood B&B and Young's Island B&B.

For more information on the association, call Pam at 612-437-3297, or write 649 W. Third St., Hastings, MN 55033.

What readers should know about...

Rates: Rates are current for '86; some may change for summer '87. Of course, all rates are subject to change.

Most of these facilities are fairly priced. A few are overpriced, in my opinion, but not many (however, if you're basing them on the European B&B model, nearly *all* are overpriced). And there are a couple of bargains, but not many. Most innkeepers are aware how their "product" compares with others, and there probably is a reason the price is so high or so low. The question becomes, can you live with that reason? (Private bathrooms are the most frequent reason for charging more; see the section on Shared Baths, next page.)

Here's a breakdown on what guests might get for their money:

$65 and up - Expect something special, such as a bottle of wine and candies on the pillow, a private bath, and perhaps a lake view or working fireplace. Privacy, rather than personal attention, is sometimes what you're buying here. There are places for people who can afford to travel this way or for a memorable honeymoon, anniversary or birthday treat.

$40-$60 - These are the places where you'll probably have the most opportunity to sit on the porch swing and talk with other guests or the owners, or have them sit at the breakfast table with you. These lodgings may be worth just as much as the higher-priced, except for one thing: perhaps they are located slightly out of town or in a town which won't support higher rates, or they have shared baths.

Under $40 - If you get what you pay for, why are they charging less? It could be they spent less on decorating and remodeling (can you live with rugs instead of carpeting, towels with frayed edges, four rooms sharing a bath, or much-less-than-elegant furnishings?). That doesn't mean the place isn't clean or otherwise OK.

Shared Baths in B&Bs: Let's be frank, OK? Don't shy away from a place just because you'll have to share a bathroom. If you were traveling in Mexico, I'd advise just the opposite. But here you'll miss some really nice places and people, not to mention lower rates, if you refuse to share.

Some people envision "shared bath" very literally, as if there were five folks in there all at once. Not the case, of course, and most often there are only two or three rooms sharing. And some of those might not be rented (especially mid-week), so you could end up with a private bath, anyway.

Innkeepers know full well the real American dream is a bathroom of one's own, and some have gone to great lengths to be able to say they offer private baths. Check this out carefully if it really matters to you. Some have added waterclosets in former bedroom closets, which results in a distinctly unusual sensation, in my opinion. Sharing means the chances are greater of having a real bath, one that's big enough to turn around in with a tub and shower and a door, not a curtain. Having a sink in the bedroom can be a big help; then there's a place to brush teeth without needing to get in the shared bathroom.

The key may be how many people you have to share with. Ask!

Have a safe and happy journey!

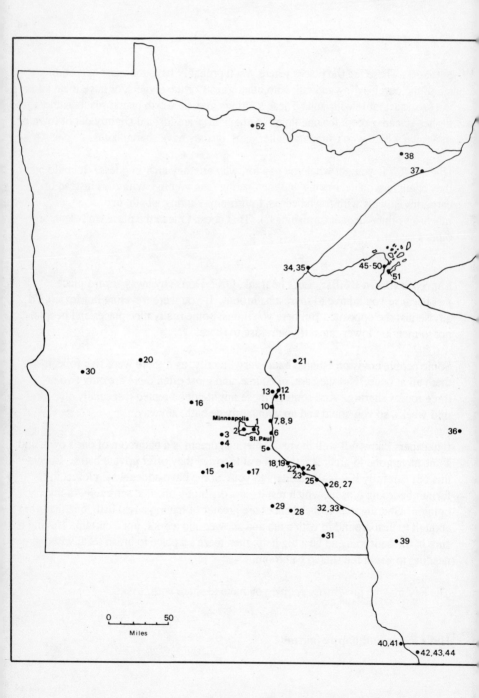

1. Chatsworth B&B - St. Paul
2. Evelo's B&B - Minneapolis
3. Christopher Inn - Excelsior
4. Bluff Creek Inn - Chaska
5. Thorwood B&B - Hastings
6. Afton House Inn - Afton
7. Driscoll's for Guests - Stillwater
8. Lowell Inn - Stillwater
9. Rivertown Inn - Stillwater
10. Asa Parker House - Marine on the St. Croix
11. St. Croix River Inn - Osceola, WI
12. Historic Taylors Falls Jail - Taylors Falls
13. Country B&B - Shafer
14. Schumacher's New Prague Hotel - New Prague
15. The Cosgrove - LeSueur
16. Thayer Hotel - Annandale
17. The Archer House - Northfield
18. Pratt-Taber Inn - Red Wing
19. St. James Hotel - Red Wing
20. Palmer House - Sauk Centre
21. Seven Pines Lodge - Lewis, WI
22. Lowell House - Old Frontenac
23. The Rahilly House - Lake City
24. Great River Farm - Stockholm, WI
25. The Anderson House - Wabasha
26. Gallery House - Alma, WI
27. Laue House - Alma, WI
28. Canterbury Inn B&B - Rochester
29. Grand Old Mansion - Mantorville
30. The American House - Morris
31. Mrs. B's Historic Lanesboro Inn - Lanesboro
32. Carriage House B&B - Winona
33. The Hotel - Winona
34. The Mansion - Duluth
35. Fitger's Inn - Duluth
36. Rosenberry Inn - Wausau, WI
37. Naniboujou Lodge - North Shore N. of Grand Marais
38. Young's Island B&B - Gunflint Trail
39. The Westby House - Westby, WI
40. The Redstone Inn - Dubuque, IA
41. The Stout House - Dubuque, IA
42. The DeSoto House Hotel - Galena, IL
43. The Farmers' Home Hotel - Galena, IL
44. Guest Houses - Galena, IL
45. Cooper Hill House - Bayfield, WI.
46. Greunke's Inn - Bayfield, WI
47. Grey Oak Guest House - Bayfield, WI
48. Le Chateau Boutin - Bayfield, WI
49. Old Rittenhouse Inn - Bayfield, WI
50. Pinehurst Inn - Bayfield, WI
51. Woods Manor B&B - LaPointe (Madeline Island), WI
52. Kettle Falls Hotel - Voyageurs National Park

Chatsworth B&B

974 Ashland
St. Paul, MN 55104
612-227-4288

Owner/Operator:
Donna Gustafson

When most of Donna and Earl Gustafson's eight children and assorted exchange students had left the nest, their three-story Victorian home in the Summit Hill neighborhood seemed awfully big and empty. Three years and many months of complete remodeling later, they found themselves in an apartment upstairs from a five-bedroom B&B.

"We wanted to stay here and we found one way we could do it," Donna said. "I really got the idea when I was looking with a group of friends for a yoga center." The realtor showing them big, older homes suggested using some of the rooms for a B&B to help finance the center. The yoga center never opened, "but the idea stuck." Chatsworth B&B opened February '86.

The house, built in 1902, had but one bathroom, so Donna and Earl looked at other homes to open a B&B. When they decided to turn their large closets into bathrooms, they were delighted to stay in their own home and have a B&B, too. Gustafsons are the fourth owners and one of the smallest families to live there, with only eight children. The second owners had 13 and the third owners had 10 children.

Guests may use the huge living room and fireplace, where the original stained glass is still in the windows. Breakfast is served in the polished birch dining room or can be eaten outside on a deck.

Rooms and Rates: Five - All on the second floor. The largest has private marble bath with double whirlpool and four-poster, lace canopy bed - $52. The other bedrooms, each with a different international theme, share two baths: one bath has a deep Japanese-style soaking tub, which fills up to the shoulders. Oriental room is in grey, red and black - $38; Scandinavian room has blue and white twin beds with down comforters - $45; Victorian room has antique bed - $38; African-Asian room is done in rattan and wicker with porch - $45. Add tax. Rates are singles; add $6 per extra person.

Meals: Breakfast only, usually juice, coffee, tea; fresh fruits; muffins, breads; yogurt and granola.

Dates open: Year 'round   **Smoking:** No

Children: Check with owner   **Pets:** No

Nearby: Governor's Residence and Summit Avenue homes, 2 blocks. Grand Avenue shops, restaurants, bus line to downtown St. Paul, 3 blocks. Grocery store.

Directions from Twin Cities: Exit I-94, go south on Lexington to Ashland, left two blocks to corner of Chatsworth.

Deposit: $25 for one-night stays; first night's deposit for longer stays

Payment: Cash, personal or traveler's checks only

Evelo's B&B

2301 Bryant Ave. S.
Minneapolis, MN 55405
612-374-9656

Owners/Operators:
Sheryl and David Evelo

Located in Minneapolis' Lowry Hill East neighborhood, this three-story home was built in 1897 for Dr. John and Kate Bell. It has had several subsequent owners, including the nearby "Miss Woods School."

"It was a dorm for about 20 years for the 'Miss Woods girls'," said Sheryl. The school was for nursery and early elementary school teacher training, and up to 25 women lived here, taking meals elsewhere.

The Evelos, both of whom are teachers in Minneapolis, bought the home in 1972 and started a B&B in 1979, believed to be the first B&B in Minnesota. "We traveled in Europe and stayed in B&Bs and we thought it was fun and interesting and a nice way to travel," Sheryl said. "The first year, I think we had one room and two guests." But publicity in the Minneapolis paper gave them a boost. Guests now include tourists, families visiting relatives in the area, students, actors, artists and businesspeople.

Downstairs, the living room, dining room and screened in front porch are "public." The first floor is done in heavy dark oak millwork and lit with antique art glass lamps. "Personally, David and I don't like going into a place that has been redone to look old," Sheryl said. The furnishings are turn-of-the-century antiques. Between Thanksgiving and New Year's, an optional "tea and goodies" is held downstairs from 4-5 p.m.

One guest room (the former maid's room) is on the second floor, and the other three rooms are on the third. Guests use the maid's stairway and have a key. A small refrigerator, coffeemaker and phone are on the third floor landing, and portable TVs are available.

Rooms and Rates: Four - All share bath with tub only on third floor, and second bath is available on first floor. All rooms are doubles, and one has an extra twin bed; rollaways are available. Singles - $25, doubles - $35, triples - $45, including tax, for third floor rooms. Maid's room on second floor is $5 less.

Meals: Breakfast varies, but Evelos are up early to buy fresh bread at small neighborhood bakeries. No meat is served. Menu may include Sherry's Egg Bake (eggs, mushrooms and cheese), fresh fruit, breads or muffins, coffee, tea and juice.

Dates open: Year 'round   **Smoking:** "If they must"

Children: Yes (crib and highchair available)   **Pets:** No

Nearby: Many restaurants within walking or bus distance. Guthrie Theatre and Walker Art Institute, Lake of the Isles, 6 blocks; Mpls. Art Institute and Children's Theatre, 11 blocks; Uptown-Calhoun Square, 8 blocks; bus to downtown, 1 block (or a 20-minute walk to downtown).

Directions from Twin Cities: Exit I-94 on Hennepin, turn left on 22nd Street (second stoplight), right on Bryant (two blocks from light).

Deposit: Not necessary

Payment: Cash, personal or traveler's checks only

Christopher Inn

201 Mill St.
Excelsior, MN 55331
612-474-6816

Owners/Operators:
Joan and Howard Johnson
Innkeeper: Cheryl Louden

A contractor, C.F. Warner, designed and built this Victorian mansion in 1887, but he couldn't find a buyer when he wanted to sell it five years later. A Minneapolis resident, James Wyer, simply traded homes with Warner. There's no telling how Warner did in the deal, but Wyer made out like a bandit. This home's front lawn then stretched two blocks to the shore of Lake Minnetonka, the perfect place for his large family.

In 1930, the house was sold to the Pearce family, which never lived in it but rented it as a duplex. It was turned in to office space in 1977. In 1985, after just one night in a B&B, Joan and Howard Johnson decided that's the type of business they'd do well and enjoy. The house was for sale; they found investors; and after less than three months of major restoration and modernization, they opened the inn in July 1985.

During the process, five bathrooms, a commercial kitchen, and a handicapped access ramp were added. New plumbing and furnace, exterior painting, new furniture and restoring original woodwork was necessary, and "every room had to be painted or wallpapered," said Howard.

Today, the inn is on the National Register of Historic Places. It has a spacious screened porch, plenty of working fireplaces, including one that burns in the dining room at breakfast, and what is believed to be the state's only grass tennis court. Guests are welcome to use it and the inn's bicycles.

During three seasons, a horse-drawn carriage is available to take guests to nearby restaurants. An afternoon tea is scheduled when the inn is full to allow guests to socialize. Small weddings and rehearsal dinners have been held on the ground floor. Provisions also available for business groups.

Meals: Breakfast is open to guests first, at about 8:30, then to the public by reservation only: Homemade breads, juice, coffee, granola, fresh fruit, plus varied entrees of seafood omelettes, seafood strata casserole, peaches and cream French toast, and Swedish apple pancakes.

Rooms and Rates: Seven - Named for Johnson family members, and the Library, with handicapped access and an antique hidden Murphy bed. It shares a full bath with the dining room - $65. Other examples: Ann's room has two twin beds, is done in cranberry, has sink in the room, shared bath - $70. David's room, table by the window, queen bed, working fireplace, a bath with shower - $105. Prices single or double. Add tax. Midweek and business discounts.

Dates open: Year 'round   **Smoking:** In designated areas

Children: In some rooms   **Pets:** No

Nearby: Two restaurants, 1 block. City Park and swimming, 4 blocks. Antique shops, downtown Excelsior, paddlewheel boat rides, 2 blocks.

Directions from Twin Cities: Highway 7 west to Excelsior. Turn left at the parking lot immediately over the bridge coming in to town.

Deposit: First night's lodging

Payment: Cash, personal or traveler's checks, VISA, MasterCard or AMEX

Bluff Creek Inn

1161 Bluff Creek Drive
Chaska, MN 55318
612-445-2735

Owner/Operator:
Marjorie Bush

"Let me live in the house by the side of the road and be a friend to man," wrote S.W. Foss. Marjorie Bush is living those words at her B&B, an 1860 brick country home.

The land, off Highway 212 east of Chaska, was granted to Chaska pioneer Joseph Vogel by President Abraham Lincoln before Minnesota was a state. Over the years, some of the land went for the highway, some for the railroad; the barns have been torn down; the house was foreclosed during the Depression, divided into a duplex, and rented for several years.

But when Bush found the house on the gravel road, she knew she wanted it for a B&B. A kindergarten teacher, former innkeeper and traveler who loves European B&Bs, she wanted to open her own B&B in the Minnesota River Valley, where she's lived for more than 20 years.

Between the time she bought the farm in February 1985 and opened the following June, "three contractors walked out on the project. Nobody wanted to do old homes," she said. Still, she had new plumbing put in, a long porch with two swings and two bedrooms added, and the summer porch restored. Wallpapering 10 rooms and stripping and varnishing she left for herself.

Guests enjoy the quiet atmosphere and swinging on the porch or tree swings. The house is carpeted and looks out over wildflowers. Breakfast is at a table by the window, served on matching Royal Doulton china and crystal. Three rooms have their own water closets (toilet and sink) curtained off and share a bathtub (an old, restored clawfoot tub she found overturned in the yard) in a separate bathroom.

Rooms: Five - Examples include: Emma's Room is in green and beige, Scandinavian antiques and Chaska brick wall, double bed - $55; Elizabeth's Room has a double, four-poster tester bed with Laura Ashley prints in green and rose; porch faces sunset, and private bath includes clawfoot tub - $85. Two room suite available in summer - $125. All prices doubles; $5 less for singles, and $5 less for second night. Add tax.

Meals: Breakfast is at 9 a.m. with juice, fresh fruit and Devonshire cream sauce, muffins or coffeecakes; Egg and Bacon Flan, Buckwheat Pancakes with Raspberry ice cream and syrup, or Peaches and Cream French Toast; dessert is blueberry grunt or bread pudding with caramel sauce. Dinners by prior arrangement.

Dates open: Year 'round

Smoking: On porches only

Children: Over 12 - ask owner

Pets: No

Nearby: Valley Fair, Canterbury Downs race track, Renaissance Festival, Murphy's Landing, Chanhassen Dinner Theater, Minnesota Landscape Arboretum, Carver Park Reserve and "494 Strip" all 10-15 minutes away.

Directions from Twin Cities: I-494 to Highway 169/212; first road on right past Highway 101 junction. House is on left.

Deposit: Full amount

Payment: Cash, personal or traveler's checks, VISA or MasterCard

Thorwood B&B

Fourth and Pine   Owners/Operators:
Hastings, MN 55033   Pam and Dick Thorsen
612-437-3297

William and Sara Thompson originally had this mansion built in 1880. Thompson was a wealthy owner of a lumber company on the Mississippi River at Hastings, just before it meets the St. Croix River.

Thompson's daughter, Kate, inherited the house, where she lived with her riverboat husband, Captain Anthony. The home was purchased in 1929 by Dr. Herman A. Fasbender, who converted it to a private hospital. An elevator was added to the third floor operating room and second floor nursery; the pharmacy was on the first floor. The hospital operated, so to speak, until about 1951, when the community's Regina Hospital was built.

When Thorsens bought the building in 1979 and named it Thorwood, it had been a six-plex apartment house since the 1950s. "We bought it thinking this is a wonderful old house. We never thought we would live in it by ourselves - it was too cut up," Pam said. Thorsens took out walls, putting rooms back to original dimensions. It's on the National Register of Historic Places.

Thorwood opened with two rooms in February '83. Today, it has five and plans call for four more. Thorsens live in the separate servant's quarters.

Thorwood is decorated with period antiques and country wallpaper. Every room has a teddy bear, courtesy of the Thorsen's two daughters. The downstairs parlor is a popular gathering place. Guests automatically receive an evening snack, but don't check out without saying goodbye - a last surprise awaits. Small groups or retreats can be accommodated.

Rooms and Rates: Five - All with private bath. Examples include: Kate's Room, double bed, done in pastels with Victorian decor, full bath - $49; The Lullaby Room, the former nursery, is done in peach and grey, queen bed, double whirlpool - $79. Capt. Anthony's Room has a four poster brass queen bed, a day bed and is done in rose and teal blue; shower only - $69. Add tax. Off-season mid-week rates and commercial rates.

22

Meals: Breakfast and evening snack. Breakfast is in a huge basket left at the door: platters of oven omelettes, hot pastries, sausages, muffins, fresh fruit, coffee, tea and juice. Snack: local wine or catawba, fruit, pastries.

Dates open: Year 'round   **Pets:** No

Smoking: In the parlor with permission of other guests

Children: Depends on circumstances - check with owners

Nearby: Downtown Hastings is a Main Street USA town, 4 blocks; walking tour between Thorwood and downtown; Levee Park, Lake Rebecca, Lock and Dam #2, fishing and boating; two ski areas.

Directions from Twin Cities: Highway 61 south to Hastings, turn right on Fourth, go to Pine. Thorwood is on the right.

Deposit: First night's lodging or confirmed by credit card

Payment: Cash, personal or traveler's checks, VISA, MasterCard or AMEX

The Afton House Inn

P.O. Box 326
Afton, MN 55001
612-436-8883

Owners/Operators:
Kathy and Gordy Jarvis
Manager: Judy Alberg

Thirty years after the first French families settled in Afton, Charles Cushing built the Cushing Hotel. The 1867 hotel opening was the second for the village of Afton; the Paterson's Hotel already had burned to the ground.

In 1907, Mary "Ma" Pennington became the owner, and the hotel's reputation as a restaurant was born. "Ma" served Sunday chicken dinners famous for miles around. The chickens were raised out in back of the restaurant, and diners knew they couldn't get anything fresher.

Over the years, other owners continued to run and expand the restaurant, but the hotel faded out. In 1976, it was purchased by Gordy and Kathy Jarvis. Gordy was chef/manager of McGuire's restaurant and Twins Motor Inn. "We wanted to bring it back to its original use, and there was a need in the area for a hotel," Gordy said. Thus began a seven-year challenge to secure needed permits for the building, listed on the National Register of Historic Places.

Finally, from Oct. 1, 1985, to April 1, 1986, the hotel was restored. The building was floodproofed and the upper floors were essentially gutted and rebuilt. New wiring, plumbing, and other major work was necessary, down to new brick sidewalks. An addition allowed the inn to have 12 rooms, instead of the original eight, and groups can be accommodated.

The hotel re-opened April 7, 1986, with the granddaughter of "Ma" Pennington present at the ceremonies.

Rooms and Rates: 12 - All with private baths, each decorated differently with antiques and reproductions in "country" wallpapers. Examples include #26 with an iron and brass double bed - $55; #29 with a four poster bed and a deck overlooking the marina and St. Croix - $95; #32 with antique twin beds, done in rose - $75. $50, $55, $65, $75, $95, and $110 doubles; some rooms slightly less singles; $10 per extra person in room. Add táx. Midweek discounts, midweek dinner and lodging packages, ski packages.

Meals: Three meals available in dining rooms on first floor.

Dates open: Year 'round   **Smoking:** 3 rooms non-smoking

Children: Yes - No charge for cribs   **Pets:** No

Nearby: St. Croix River marinas and dockage, gift shops, ice cream parlor, toy shop, 1-2 blocks. Shopping center, 2 miles. Downhill ski area, 4 miles.

Directions from Twin Cities: I-94 east to Highway 95, south four miles to Afton, continue straight on County Rd. 21 when 95 turns to right. Inn is on the left at the corner.

Deposit: First night's lodging

Payment: Cash, personal or traveler's checks, VISA, MasterCard or AMEX

Driscoll's for Guests

1103 S. Third St.
Stillwater, MN 55082
612-439-7486

Owner/Operator:
Mina Driscoll

This Victorian single-family home is one of Stillwater's oldest, built just after the Civil War by a dentist who worked downtown. Though that was just a half-mile away, his home bordered the very edge of development in this St. Croix River town, and his property was literally at road's end.

For three winters, he experimented with a gravity furnace when most people used stoves, said Mina Driscoll. The house was so cold his wife took her daughter to what is now the Lowell Inn for most of those winters. The three Swedish servants stayed at the home and suffered through.

Samuel Clewell, who owned several newspapers including what is now the Stillwater Gazette, also owned the house. Driscoll is the fifth owner. A screened porch was added after the Spanish-American War, but the structure is otherwise unaltered. The original rosewood, pine and walnut woodwork remains, carved by Swedish carpenters who worked without blueprints.

Driscoll thought of doing a B&B years ago. "I've been staying in them for 20-some years," mostly in England and Ireland. "I go over there to bicycle and I found I met all the interesting people in B&Bs." She opened officially in spring '85 (she started earlier but got few guests. "Nobody had heard of them.")

Converting the home to a B&B involved redecorating and adding a bathroom. Family antiques, reproductions and wicker are used with other "country" and Victorian furnishings. Guests are free to use the parlor, with a working fireplace and piano, and a screened porch. They are served tea upon arrival. Guests in the Rose Room have a private entry and key.

Rooms and Rates: Three - Rose Room, done in rose tones with a double bed, has private bath/clawfoot tub, no shower. Winnie the Pooh Room, named after a daughter's teddy bear, has huge antique double bed. A third room has king-sized waterbed, shares bath with tub and shower with Winnie Room. July through Oct., Rose Room - $55, Winnie and Waterbed rooms - $47. Nov. through June, Rose Room - $45, Winnie and Waterbed rooms - $40. Add tax. Midweek discounts.

Meals: Breakfast is served at the guests' leisure in rooms or on the porch and includes quiche or omelettes; cheese and fruit plate; homemade popovers, raisin or banana bread; coffee, tea and juice.

Dates open: Year 'round

Smoking: Not in rooms

Children: Yes

Pets: Yes

Nearby: Downtown Stillwater shops, restaurants, winery, antique shops, 6 blocks; St. Croix River, 8 blocks; tennis courts, 3 blocks.

Directions from Twin Cities: Highway 36 east to Fourth Street, turn left. Go to Hancock, turn right 1 block to corner of Third and Hancock.

Deposit: Half of room rate

Payment: Cash, personal or traveler's checks only

Lowell Inn

102 N. Second
Stillwater, MN 55082
612-439-1100

Owners/Operators:
Maureen and Arthur Palmer

Arthur Palmer was literally born into innkeeping. His parents, Nelle and Arthur, Sr., opened the Lowell Inn under their management on Christmas Day 1930, and it has remained in the family since. Nelle had been one of the Obrecht Sisters, a family acting company, and she met and married pianist Arthur while traveling the Midwest as they produced live theater. Tired of living on the road and concerned about their future as talking movies became popular, they jumped at the chance to manage the Lowell Inn.

Adding little touches of collectibles and antiques helped draw guests on the back roads to the faraway village of Stillwater. In 1945, the Palmers were able to purchase the inn. While both his parents have passed on, Art Palmer and Maureen, his wife, have raised most of their nine children on innkeeping traditions.

Originally, Stillwater's lumber barons wheeled and dealed in the Sawyer House, a luxury hotel built in 1848. It was demolished in 1924 in order to build the Lowell Inn. The Williamsburg design is said to resemble Mount Vernon and the original 13 colonies are represented with flags and 13 white pillars. Change at the Lowell Inn will continue: Palmer plans to fill the entire block with a complex of additional rooms and meeting facilities.

Rooms and Rates: 21 - All on the second and third floors, with private baths, complimentary bar or wine, and a ceramic cat on the bed; most done in opulent provincial antiques or reproductions with a stereo system. Four bridal/anniversary rooms have round double whirlpools - $119. Four bridal/anniversary rooms have round showers - $99. Six have kings - $89. Four have queens - $79. Two are called "petite queens," though the lavender room is big - $69. The Nelle Suite has a living room and an inlaid games board, queen bed - $109. Prices doubles or singles. Add tax.

Meals: Lunch and dinner available in dining rooms (no room service).

Dates open: Year 'round   **Smoking:** Yes

Children: "Welcome"   **Pets:** No

Nearby: Downtown Stillwater gift shops, restaurants, winery, antique shops, 1-4 blocks; St. Croix River, 3 blocks.

Directions from Twin Cities: Highway 36 east to Stillwater, follow signs downtown; turn left on Myrtle at second stoplight, go 1 block to Second St., turn right.

Deposit: Full amount

Payment: Cash, personal or traveler's checks, VISA, MasterCard, AMEX or Diners Club

The Rivertown Inn

306 W. Olive Street
Stillwater, MN 55082
612-430-2955

Owner/Operator:
Judy Anderson

John O'Brien was one of Stillwater's most prosperous lumbermen when he had this home built for his family on the corner of Fifth and Olive streets, high above the St. Croix River.

But over the years, such a large home could not be maintained just for one family. In the 1940s, it became a tri-plex. When Dick and Judy Anderson bought it in 1976, they restored it and used it for their home, plus for an emergency shelter home for foster children and, later, a girl's group home. Its three floors lent itself well to plenty of inhabitants.

Dick added antique pot-bellied and Franklin stoves to several of the rooms. Four rooms also have working fireplaces. Pieces of fireplaces, original chandeliers and woodwork were found in the carriage house, which they put back in the main house.

Once again a single-family home and one of Stillwater's Victorian mansions, the home was turned into a B&B in 1981 by the next owners. Judy is now the third innkeeper. "My inlaws had a motel, so I got some training there, and I'm learning as I go along," said the Stillwater teacher. "I'm meeting some nice people." Her family assists her.

Guests have use of the first floor's living and dining rooms, a large screened porch with swings, and a gazebo in the yard. Antique furniture is used, including a large hotel desk in the parlor, where guests check in.

Rooms and Rates: Nine - Eight of which are decorated in Victorian style; two with private bath. Examples include: John O'Brien Room, dark wood, double antique bed, fireplace, done in blues and reds, private half-bath - $60 weekends, $45 weekdays; Faith's Room, done in blue and white, double brass bed, fireplace, private bath with tub only - $60/$45; Teresa's Room on third floor, attic room done in pink with a white iron queen bed, shared bath with woodrimmed clawfoot tub with shower - $35/$20. Add tax.

Meals: Breakfast is served informally, continental-European style, in the dining room from 8 - 10:30, and includes juice and coffee; hard rolls with cheese and jellies; muffins.

Dates open: Year 'round

Smoking: Designated areas

Children: Check with owner

Pets: No

Nearby: Downtown shops, restaurants, caves, antique shops, 3 blocks; St. Croix River with paddlewheel cruise, 4 blocks; tennis courts, x-c and downhill skiing, bike trails.

Directions from Twin Cities: Highway 36 east to downtown Stillwater, turn left on Olive Street at intersection before first stoplight, go up hill to Fifth. Inn is on the corner.

Deposit: Half of room rate

Payment: Cash, personal or traveler's checks, VISA or MasterCard

Asa Parker House

17500 St. Croix Trail North
Marine on the St. Croix,
MN 54047
612-433-5248

Owner/Operator:
Ivonne Cuendet

When Ivonne Cuendet opened her B&B in July, the plumber was barely on his way out when guests were on their way in. Work was done at breakneck speed between May 1 and the July 18 arrival of guests, who wanted to hold a family reunion in her B&B. "They told me I had contributed to their memories, and I thought, 'Oh, this *is* like a Walton house,' " she said, referring to the TV Walton family's closeness.

The compliment on the hominess of this 1856 building by her first guests was heady stuff for Cuendet, who has thought about running a B&B for years and finally took the plunge alone in late 1985. "I always had the sense that if the right house came around I should do it."

Originally, the "right house" was built by Asa Parker, the Vermont lumberman who brought the lumber industry up the St. Croix River from Stillwater. He and Isabella, his wife, had servants, and Cuendet now lives in those quarters. His house was modeled after a stately Vermont home.

Cuendet is the fifth owner of the home, which is in Marine's National Historic District. An 88-year-old neighbor grew up in the house. He watched with interest as Cuendet patched, sanded and wallpapered walls, rewired, added three bathrooms, carpeted, put in a new fence and sidewalks, and replaced 26 windows. Local craftspeople helped with everything from mouldings and sewing curtains to brochure design. Guests have use of a double parlor with a fire in the woodstove and a grand piano, the dining room, and lighted private tennis court.

Rooms and Rates: Five - Three with private baths. Examples: Jardin Room is former library, done in blues, queen bed, original clawfoot tub and pedestal sink - $84. Fur Elise overlooks river valley, has wood burning stove, white iron queen bed, private bath with shower - $84. Fleur is attic room with sloping ceiling, double bed, has private balcony, shared bath - $64. Add tax.

Meals: Breakfast is in dining room from 8-9:30 and includes juice, tea or coffee on the porch or in parlor, fruit such as baked apple with custard sauce; baked egg with havarti cheese, cinnamon French toast or cheese blintz, with cold fruit and hot croissant.

Dates open: Year 'round

Smoking: "Discouraged"

Children: No

Pets: No, but kennel nearby

Nearby: Village of Marine, shops and ice cream parlor, 2 blocks; marina and canoe rental, 1/2 mile; bike trail Stillwater-Taylors Falls outside door; lighted tennis court and gazebo in back. Adjacent to William O'Brien State Park.

Directions from Twin Cities: I-94 or Highway 36 to Stillwater, then Highway 95 to Marine on the St. Croix. Turn left on County Road 4, turn right on Fifth Street, follow signs.

Deposit: First night's lodging

Payment: Cash, personal or traveler's checks, VISA or MasterCard

St. Croix River Inn

305 River Street
Osceola, WI 54020
715-294-4248

Owner/Operator:
Robert G. Marshall
Innkeeper: Margy Rogers

Robert Marshall, a Minneapolis developer, and his investors are only the second "family" to own this Dutch Colonial building. It was constructed in the early 1900s of stone from a quarry just south of Osceola, then a lumber town making commercial use of the St. Croix River.

The home was built by C.W. and May Staples. Staples was the son of a New Hampshire man who was a miller, merchant and drug store owner in booming Osceola. Staples was born in Illinois in 1852 and moved to Osceola with his parents when he was only 3. He attended local schools and moved to Menomonie, Wis., to serve as a bookkeeper, but returned to join his father at the drug store.

May and C.W. Staples had a daughter, Irene, who also became a druggist. For many years, Irene Staples Cooper lived in the stone house overlooking the river. She moved and sold the house to Marshall in 1984.

Marshall's first plans were to turn the thick-walled structure into a condominium on three levels. But he and his architect nixed those plans, and a B&B inn eventually resulted. Extensive renovation involved additions outside the original stone exterior walls, and some of those stone walls are now interior walls.

Suites are named after steamboats built at Osceola and are done in antique reproductions. A game room on the top floor is decorated like a riverboat wheelhouse; a lobby is also for guests' use. Guests find heavy terry robes hanging in the wardrobe. Riverview rooms have either a balcony or patio with chairs, and three have whirlpools at window level for a river view while soaking.

Rooms and Rates: Seven - All with private baths with whirlpools and six with hand-held showers; queen beds. Examples: G.B. Knapp - four-poster canopy bed, plus river view room - $150. Maggie Reaney - four-poster bed - $85. Jennie Hays - four-poster canopy bed, huge cathedral riverview windows - $125. Nellie Kent and Minnie Will - two poster beds, riverview whirlpools, patios - $100. Osceola - "apartment" - $150. Add tax. Midweek discounts.

Meals: Breakfast is served to the guest rooms; includes sweet rolls, muffins, juice, fruit, coffee; hot breakfast on weekends includes quiche.

Dates open: Year 'round

Smoking: Designated areas only

Children: No

Pets: No

Nearby: Shops, restaurants, bars, waterfalls in Osceola, 2-4 blocks. Downhill skiing at two hills, 8-10 minutes; x-c skiing, hiking Interstate State Park, 10 minutes; x-c skiing, hiking William O'Brien State Park, 10 minutes; canoeing St. Croix at Taylor's Falls, 10 minutes.

Directions from Twin Cities: Highway 36 to Stillwater; north on Highway 95 to Highway 243; or take I-35E north to Highway 97, east to Highway 95. Turn right (east) and cross river on Highway 243 to Osceola; turn left on the main street through town, then left on Third Ave.; drive by hospital and church. Inn is on the left/riverside.

Deposit: First night's lodging

Payment: Cash, personal or traveler's checks, VISA or MasterCard

35

Historic Taylors Falls Jail

102 Government Road
Taylors Falls, MN 54084
612-465-3112

Owner/Operator:
Helen White

"Painter Beck, who got drunk Tuesday night, went to sleep on the front porch of Mrs. Guard's residence and woke up yesterday morning in jail." - Taylors Falls Journal, June 16, 1881.

These days, when people wake up in the Taylors Falls jail, they remember how they got there, and they got there on purpose.

The jail, well over 100 years old, has been restored by Helen White as a 16 x 24 foot bed and breakfast "home," with a complete kitchen, loft bedroom, full bathroom and living room.

Listed on the National Register of Historic Places, the jail belongs to White as part of her property and house next door. What does one do with a jail in one's yard? "I had the building and knew I was going to restore it. There wasn't any good use for it except as a storage building, and that would've been a shame." Since it was the local lock-up, it has been a garage, a shoe repair shop, an ice house and a shop in which dog sleds were built.

"I was thinking about an apartment," she said, but "the architect said, 'What a pity more people can't enjoy it.' " White gutted the interior and started over, restoring the outside based on historic photos. The result was a B&B, which opened in 1981.

Guests are much more comfortable than those who first frequented one of the four cells. Two-by-fours have been installed as room dividers and ceilings to suggest the original cells, also made of 2 x 4s. Local artists and craftspeople have helped with everything from design to the iron steps and railings, the wood stove restoration and the pottery. It's heated both with wood and electricity. A cross-stitch kit with the jail design is given weekend guests.

Rooms and Rates: One loft double bed for 2, and one sofabed, also sleeping two. Bath has both tub and shower. $55 doubles. Weekends, two nights $110, third night free. $10 per extra person; four maximum. Add tax.

Meals: Breakfast fixings are in the refrigerator. Guests grind their own coffee and make juice, eggs, pancakes with local maple syrup, or have fruit, cereal, cheese and rolls.

Dates open: Year 'round   **Smoking:** Yes

Children: Yes, but limit is four people   **Pets:** No

Nearby: Folsum House museum and Angels Hill Historic District, excursion boats, Interstate Park headquarters, shops and restaurants, 1-2 blocks; two canoe rentals, 1 mile.

Directions from Twin Cities: I-35 to Taylors Falls/Highway 8; at bottom of hill, turn left, come up hill one block, turn left on Government Road. Jail is on right.

Deposit: Full amount

Payment: Cash, personal or traveler's checks only

Country B&B

32030 Ranch Trail
Shafer, MN 55074
612-257-4773

Owners/Operators:
Lois and Budd Barott

Country B&B is where Lois Barott shares her childhood years of growing up in the country with city folks who come to visit. There's a porch swing, fresh eggs from the chicken coop, and a big dog who loves to retrieve sticks. There's a country lane for walking, birds sing and the atmosphere is peaceful and relaxing. This is how an imagined house in the country would be.

Lois Barott grew up with a brother and sister on these 60 country acres. Her parents had milk cows and they raised corn, oats, hay and soybeans. She and Budd raised their six children on the same property. For years, Budd commuted 138 miles a day to his job, and for some of those years, Lois joined him. She had a job soldering computer boards "when I got tired of milking the cows." After awhile, though, milking looked pretty good compared to that commute.

"I used to sit at work and think, 'There must be something else I can do,'" Lois said. After the last child left home, she quit her job and began toying with the idea of opening a B&B. Budd took early retirement and told her they ought to sell the house because it cost to much to heat for two people. Budd said that within a month, Lois had researched B&Bs and was determined to turn their home into one.

Their brick farmhouse was built in 1882 by Swedish immigrant Lars Thorsander. Renovation before opening the B&B included a new foundation, rewiring, reinsulating and reroofing, and adding trim and a deck in back. Three upstairs bedrooms became the guest rooms, a bath was added, and an attic became a sitting and reading room. Lois wallpapered and made comforters and cushions for the wicker furniture.

Rooms and Rates: All rooms have wicker furniture and handmade comforters and cushions. The Little Room ($31.80) has a double bed and shares a bath (modern tub and shower) with the Lavender Room ($58.30), a large room that looks out over the front lawn and has a queen bed. The Green Room ($47.70) has a double bed and private bath with a clawfoot tub. Prices are for doubles or singles and include tax.

Meals: Breakfast is family style and includes ham, bacon or sausage; Budd's omelettes with fresh eggs; Lois' buttermilk pancakes with homemade maple syrup; fresh fruit; hashbrowns from scratch and sometimes homemade bread with homemade jams and jellies; Swedish egg coffee, tea, milk and juices. Guests can sit at the large kitchen table and talk while Barotts cook.

Dates open: Year 'round   **Smoking:** No

Children: 12 and older   **Pets:** No

Nearby: St. Croix boat rides and canoeing in Taylors Falls, 5 mi. Wild River State Park for hiking, x-c skiing, 5 mi. Sunrise River tubing, 9 mi. Fishing, boating on Chisago area lakes, 3 mi. Snowmobile on Scandia Trail in Center City, 2 mi. Museums, pottery shops, flea markets, antique shops.

Directions from Twin Cities: I-35 to Forest Lake Highway 8 exit, continue east through Center City to Shafer. Turn left on Co. Rd. 21 through town, continue past Co. Rd. 82, watch for Ranch Trail. Turn left, go about one mile. House is visible around the bend on the left.

Deposit: Full amount

Payment: Cash, personal or traveler's checks only

Schumacher's New Prague Hotel

212 W. Main St.
New Prague, MN 56071
612-758-2133
Metro Line: 454-7285

Owners/Operators:
John and Kathleen Schumacher

When John Schumacher, an executive chef with Marriott Hotel Corp., was transferred to the Twin Cities in 1974, he soon realized a lifelong ambition. "I discovered a sleeping beauty and found my chance to achieve the all-American dream -- owning my own business," he said. He found the New Prague Hotel, a small hotel designed by Cass Gilbert, the architect of the state Capitol.

The 1898 building was in a state of disrepair and had been for sale for more than five years. "I offered the owner $3,000 down on a contract for deed and she accepted." Schumacher left Marriott and devoted all his energies to creating this restaurant, capitalizing on his German heritage and the Czechoslovakian heritage of New Prague.

The hotel originally served traveling salesmen who used the nearby railroad for transportation. "When I bought the hotel, rooms rented for $2.50-$12.50 per night and showers could be taken for $1 in what is now the sitting room," he said. Schumacher remodeled, creating 12 sleeping rooms furnished with Bavarian folk-painted furniture by artist Pipka, and down comforters, linens and lighting from Europe. A complimentary bottle of German wine and candy tucked into the pillows await guests.

The media soon discovered the hotel, and articles and television spots contributed to its widening repution. The hotel is well known for its cuisine and unique atmosphere. Schumacher and Kathleen, his wife, actively run the business and frequently are on the premises to visit with guests.

Rooms and Rates: 12, named for the months - $65, 75 and 85, plus tax. May is the room with ladder to the canopy bed, handpainted clawfoot tub (no shower) - $85 (July is similar at $75). April, the most popular room, has round king bed, Victorian furnishings, tub, shower and bar - $85. June has twin beds built in a wood frame along the wall for head-to-head or toe-to-toe sleeping, shower, and Swiss Alps decor - $65. $5 less single occupancy; 25 percent discounts Sunday-Thursday.

Meals: Breakfast is available to hotel guests all week, open to public only on weekends. Lunch and dinner served daily.

Dates open: Year 'round   **Smoking:** Yes

Children: Yes, but discouraged   **Pets:** No

Nearby: Canoe Minnesota River, 9 miles; x-c skiing, 18-hole golf course, near town; tennis, movie theater, shopping in town.

Directions from Twin Cities: I-35W to Highway 101/169 to Jordan, Highway 21 to New Prague; I-35 south to Highway 19, west to New Prague.

Deposit: Full amount

Payment: Cash, personal or traveler's checks only

The Cosgrove

228 S. Second St.
LeSueur, MN 56058
612-665-2763

Owners/Operators:
Pat and Paul Sullivan

Carson Cosgrove had this house built as his own in 1893, when he was a hardware store owner who dealt in farm machinery. He and other businessmen decided what LeSueur, a farming town located in the fertile Minnesota River valley, really needed at the time was a corn packing plant, so he became one of the founders of the Minnesota Valley Canning Co.

Later, one of that company's research biologists developed a sweet pea bigger even than the LeSueur pea, and it was named "Green Giant." Today, the company Cosgrove founded is named after that pea.

As the fourth owners, Pat and Paul Sullivan purchased the National Register home in July 1984 with the idea of doing a B&B in the back of their minds. "We thought we'd have an adventure through the B&B," Paul said, and it opened in May 1985. The house had been cut into rental property in the 1940s, then done over in the '60s, and the original woodwork was still intact.

The walls are loaded with artwork: "Pat collects, I appreciate," Paul says. Food is an important experience here; Pat graduated from the Hennepin Vo-Tech as a trained chef. At 6 p.m., guests gather in the dining room for wine, spring water and hors d'oeuvres, including puffed pastry filled with feta cheese, Coquille St. Jacques, smoked oysters or cheeses. Guests find a late-night snack inside their room, perhaps of fresh grapes, carrot cake and amaretto.

Sullivans also open up their 40 acres of woods on Rush River Ridge for guests to picnic or to use a day cabin, or to get the Sullivans to guide wildflower or morel mushroom hunts. (The morels end up in omelettes later.) Guests may use a sunporch in back of the house, dining and living rooms and front porch.

Rooms and Rates: Four, only three of which are rented at once because of shared bath, with tub and shower. Meg's Room has a porch which can be reached by climbing out the window/door, double bed - $60. Rob's Room is done in red, white and blue theme, iron bed, fireplace - $55. Amy's Room is octagonal, has lace parasol canopy over bed, done in yellows - $50. Bradford's Room has fireplace, queen bed, done in green and peach - $65. Add tax.

Meals: Breakfast is at 9:30 "or by group consensus," on linen in the dining room or in bed. Newspaper and coffee are served to rooms. Breakfast may include Eggs Cosgrove (artichoke heart bottom, puree of pea, deviled egg, mornay sauce baked with parmesan), Strudel Shepard (egg-based strudel baked with meat); bacon and fresh fruits; juice, coffee and tea.

Dates open: Weekends year 'round; weeknights by special arrangement

Smoking: Yes (owners do)   **Pets:** No

Children: Over 12 only and in room of their own

Nearby: Hiking and morel hunting on Sullivan's property, 2.5 mi.; x-c skiing, golf, 2-3 mi; antique shopping, 2 blocks and in Minn. River Valley; Sakatah bike trail, 25 mi.

Directions from Twin Cities: I-494 south to Highway 169 southwest to LeSueur; follow exits to downtown. Second Street is two blocks from there.

Deposit: $25

Payment: Cash, personal or traveler's checks only

43

Thayer Hotel

Highway 55
Annandale, MN 55302
612-274-3371

Owner/Operator:
Wally Houle

Many of the towns which were situated along the midwest's rail lines did not just spring up. Residents had to plead with and sometimes pay railroads to make a stop on their land, which would allow a town to survive.

In 1895, A.A. (Gus) Thayer did it the other way around -- the Soo Line Railroad actually paid *him* to build a hotel in Annandale, and gave him the land, besides. Thayer was manager of the Pleasant Lake Hotel across the street, but it burned down. The railroad found Annandale a key stop for prairie passengers' comfort, and wanted to promote resorting and fishing by Twin Citians. "Tourism was unheard of before that," said Wally Houle. "Soo Line advertised excursion fares for the weekend of $1.75 round trip." The hotel was "pretty classy" with its wild west balconies.

Houle didn't have it so good -- he had to buy the place. He was mayor of Annandale when the hotel was up for sale. The city wanted to preserve the structure, listed on the National Register of Historic Places, so, when no buyer was found, the city bought the hotel. Eight years and no buyer later, Houle decided to restore it himself.

For seven months, five carpeneters plus other contractors worked more than full time for a May 1985 opening. "We took everything down to the bare walls, except in the lobby, where we worked around the tin walls and ceiling," Houle said. A total of 14 rooms now stand where 22 once did, all with original furniture or antiques and Victorian country decor.

From mid-December through mid-March, expect weekend packages that include meals and a sleigh ride. Other old-fashioned extras include churning ice cream (3 flavors) and cutting and aging their beef.

Rooms: 14 - All with private bath with pull-chain toilets and clawfoot tubs; shared shower available. Queen beds in four, rest doubles. Examples include: Room 202 - white iron queen bed in pink, white and green - $50 summers; Room 201 - 1865 double bed with burled walnut headboard - $60 summer; Bridal Suite with double wedding ring quilt on queen canopy bed - $75.

Meals: Breakfast is included in the room rate; order anything off the menu. Three meals available in restaurant.

Dates open: Year 'round

Smoking: Yes

Children: Yes (cots available)

Pets: Check with owner

Nearby: Minnesota Pioneer Park, 1.5 miles; city park with swimming, 6 blocks; shopping, 2-4 blocks; down hill and groomed x-c ski trails, 1 mile; 25 lakes within 5 miles.

Directions from Twin Cities: Highway 55 to Annandale, hotel on right

Rates: Rooms $50 summer, $45 fall, $40 winter; suites $60, $55 and $50; Bridal Suite $75, $70, $65. Midweek rates 10 percent less. Single occupancy $5 less. Add tax.

Deposit: $20

Payment: Cash, personal or traveler's checks, VISA or MasterCard

The Archer House

212 Division St.
Northfield, MN 55057
507-645-5661
Minn. toll-free 1-800-247-2235

Owner/Operator:
Dallas Haas
General Manager:
Mary Lethbridge

Described in the local press as "an episode of the grandest proportion in Northfield's history," the opening of the 50-room Archer House in 1877 drew three brass bands, as well as the local band. Today, the French Second Empire brick hotel on the Cannon River still draws out-of-towners.

In the years between, the hotel traded hands at least 31 times. It was known as the Manawa, Hotel Ball and the Stuart Hotel, but it always operated as a hotel. Haas restored the original name when he bought it in 1981.

And Haas has done more than restore a name. Originally, he renovated a small mall on one side of the hotel and had no interest in the hotel itself. But the mall generated business which used the hotel's parking lot and property, prompting the suggestion than Haas simply buy the hotel, too.

After he agreed, "reality set in," he said. Not only did he get a 30-room hotel with only 20 rooms operational, but the Jefferson Bus office and retail space were included in the deal. "Basically, nothing had been done to the rooms since the '50s," said Manager Mary Lethbridge, herself a former owner. A massive renovation was in order.

Downstairs, a tavern and restaurant serve three meals a day. A deli and retail shops are open on the ground floor. Only two rooms have been lost in the changes on the second and third floors. All decor is "country," with handmade quilts and decorations. Meeting rooms have been added. Guests in suites receive complimentary wine or champagne and handpainted, personalized wine glasses.

Rooms and Rates: 28 rooms, $40-95. Each has its own design and name. All double or queen beds. All have baths, some shower or tub only, some with bathroom partially enclosed in room. Stuart Room has pattern of old hotel in quilt, hand stencils on wall, shower only - $45. Bridal suite has four poster bed, double wedding ring quilt on queen bed, single whirlpool - $90. Anniversary suite has round double whirlpool, white iron queen bed - $90. Several other suites available. Add tax. Midweek discount.

Meals: Guests receive morning coffee and newspaper. Deli and restaurant on premises.

Dates open: Year 'round

Smoking: Yes

Children: Yes - no extra charge

Pets: No

Nearby: Downtown shops and restaurants; Cannon River waterfall, Northfield Historical Society Museum (former bank where Jesse James gang shot), historic tours, Northfield Arts Guild productions, 2 blocks. Hiking, cross-country skiing, Carleton and St. Olaf college activities, 5-10 minutes.

Directions from Twin Cities: I-35W south about 35 miles to Highway 19 East. Continue to Division Street, turn left on Division. Hotel on left.

Deposit: First night's lodging

Payment: Cash, personal or traveler's checks, VISA or MasterCard

The Pratt-Taber Inn

706 W. Fourth
Red Wing, MN 55066
612-388-5945

Owners/Operators:
   Jan and Darrel Molander

When W.A. Pratt, one of Red Wing's first bankers, built a home in 1876, he spared no detail. Butternut woodwork with fancy fretwork was included, as was feather painting on slate fireplaces throughout the 13-room Italianate building. Yet the cost was $4,000. His daughter, a Taber by marriage, lived in the home until 1952, when it was made into apartments.

When the building later went up for sale, a realtor who was aware of the B&B movement contacted the Molanders and told them about the home's possibilities. "My husband had the know-how and I had the ideas, so we put it all together," said Jan, an interior designer. Though they'd never even stayed in a B&B, they went into a partnership and began work for an August opening. "Massive cleaning" and wallpapering, replumbing, rebuilding the foundation and porch, and removing a wall that plastered shut an opening to the dining room were among the necessary improvements to the home, listed on the National Register of Historic Places.

Guests get a personal tour soon after check-in. One of the first things they learn is that there is coffee, lemonade, cider, cookies, donuts or pretzels always available in a bright kitchen with antique butler's cabinets. "I find that the kitchen is the thing that makes people feel most at home," Jan said. They also can use the sitting room, piano and library, provided the library is not rented as part of a three-room suite, which has a unique antique Murphy bed hidden in what appears to be a buffet.

Jan can explain the history of the antiques in each room. Look for uncommon attention to details, like an old-fashioned collar placed in a drawer or a Victorian woman's shoes on the floor. Special provisions for business groups.

Meals: Breakfast is served in the dining room from 8:30 to 10 a.m. or on the porch in the summer, and includes homemade blueberry or apple coffee cakes, raisin bran or apple spice mini muffins, sausage roll-ups, fresh fruit platter, juice, coffee, teas and hot chocolate. Snacks also available.

Rooms and Rates: Six - Named for Pratt family members; plus the Library, which can sleep 8 in a 3-room suite for $150. Examples include: Henrietta's Room, antique double bed nearly nine feet high, open deck off side door - $69; Aunt Aggie's Room, antique queen white iron bed, wicker dressing table, private sink - $59. Each two rooms share one full bath. Downstairs, Matilda's Room - $49; Etta's Room - $79, plus Library. Prices are doubles. Add tax.

Dates open: Year 'round

Children: If quiet, well-behaved

Smoking: Yes

Pets: Has outdoor area for dogs

Nearby: Levee Park, downtown, riverboat and trolley car, 3 blocks. Trolley picks up guests at house in summer; horse and buggy service from house on summer weekends. Antiquing, golfing, skiing, pottery shopping.

Directions from Twin Cities: Highway 61 south to Red Wing, turn right on Dakota, two blocks to Fourth. House is on right-hand corner.

Deposit: First night's lodging

Payment: Cash, personal or traveler's checks, VISA or MasterCard

The St. James Hotel

406 Main St.
Red Wing, MN 55066
612-388-2846
Twin Cities line 227-1800

Owners:
Red Wing Shoe Company
Manager:
Gene Foster

In the 1870s, Red Wing claimed to be the largest wheat market in the world, shipping the gold grain down the river to hungry ports. Eleven businessmen built the first-class St. James Hotel in 1875, and it was heralded by newspapers and residents as an exceptional dining and lodging facility. It's now on the National Register of Historic Places.

As ownership changed, the Lillyblad family purchased the hotel and managed it for 72 years. Clara Lillyblad's cooking was reportedly so good that passenger trains made a special stop in Red Wing for a meal at "Clara's."

The hotel operated continuously until 1977, when the Red Wing Shoe Company purchased it and began extensive renovation to return it to its 1875 glory. Some original fixtures were discovered in the basement, the stairway was returned to its original place, and photographs of riverboats that docked in Red Wing became the source of names for the rooms.

"As with most older hotels, it had undergone so many furniture changes there really was not much that was useable," said Kathy Johnson, marketing manager. Antiques were hunted up, quilts were sewn for the beds, and each of the 41 rooms was designed individually.

When the shoe company re-opened the hotel again in 1979, it sported a shopping mall, a parking ramp, meeting and banquet rooms and three cafes and dining rooms. Another section was added in 1981 for 19 more rooms, though these rooms are as reminiscent of the late 1800s as the others.

This is a full-service hotel with bellboys, elevators and turndown service. Guests receive complimentary champagne or Catawba juice on arrival and coffee, tea or hot chocolate in the morning, plus weekday paper.

Rooms: 60 - Each with its own decor and private bath, and usually with writing tables. Expect brass, white iron or antique wood beds, and small floral or early American print wallpaper, coordinating handmade quilts and carpet. About half have a river view; 57 have both tub and shower.

Meals: Three meals a day available in ground floor dining rooms and cafe, special Sunday brunch.

Dates open: Year 'round   **Smoking:** Yes

Children: Yes (18 and under free in room)   **Pets:** No

Nearby: Levee Park (riverboat and cable car depart from park in summer), 1 block. Sheldon Memorial Auditorium, 2 blocks; YMCA, 1/2 block.

Directions from Twin Cities: Highway 61 south to Red Wing. Hotel is on left side of Main Street; turn left at stoplight by hotel to parking lot.

Rates: $55, $70, $85 (some with single whirlpools), and $98.50 (suites with double whirlpools), singles or doubles. Most rooms are $70 with queen beds. Add tax. Midweek discounts.

Deposit: First night's lodging or confirmed by credit card

Payment: Cash, personal or traveler's checks, VISA, MasterCard, Discover, AMEX, Diners Club or Carte Blanche

Palmer House Hotel

500 Sinclair Lewis Ave.
(at Main Street, of course)
Sauk Centre, MN 56378
612-352-3431

Owners/Operators:
Al Tingley and
Richard Schwartz

The Palmer House Hotel was built in 1901, a year before Sinclair Lewis was hired there. As the story goes, co-owner Al Tingley says, the young author-to-be spent a lot of time daydreaming and reading on the job. He finally was fired after he forgot to awaken a guest in time to catch a train.

The hotel is on the National Register of Historic Places and has reappeared in three books - as the Minniemashie House in "Main Street," as the American House in "Work of Art," and in "Corner on Main Street," the true story of innkeepers on Sinclair Lewis Avenue, which Tingley wrote.

Tingley is upfront about guests not getting "country" wallpapers with grapevine wreaths on the wall. "We wanted to keep the place as much like the original hotel as we could," and that includes baths down the hall. He and Schwartz have redone 25 of the 37 rooms, little by little, in what has not been an easy or cheap job. When they bought the hotel in 1974, it was in much worse condition than they expected, with major repairs and upgrading necessary, such as hoisting the building four inches to put in new footings.

The red oak lobby is the same as Lewis saw, as is the staircase. Twenty rooms have writing tables Mr. Palmer himself bought for use by traveling salesmen. Light switches, however, could hardly be originals. "It was the first hotel outside Minneapolis to have running water and electricity," Tingley said. "The light switches were worn out in six months because people kept turning them on and off so much." Tingley and Schwartz have done most of the work themselves; Tingley is a gourmet cook and handles the restaurant business while Schwartz is the hotel man.

Rooms and Rates: 37 - All with sinks in rooms, furnished with antiques; three have private baths. Bath down hall for other rooms has original clawfoot tub. Also shower room. Rooms are usually with double beds. Rooms with bath down the hall - $19. Rooms with private bath - $25. Rooms with two twin beds, private bath - $35. Add tax.

Meals: Three meals available in restaurant. Dining room opens at 7 a.m.

Dates open: Year 'round

Smoking: Designated areas

Children: Yes

Pets: Yes

Nearby: Sinclair Lewis' boyhood home, 3 blocks; lake and park, 1 block; theater, shopping, next door-2 blocks.

Directions from Twin Cities: I-94 northwest to Sauk Centre exit, turn right and head downtown; hotel on left.

Deposit: $10

Payment: Cash, personal or traveler's checks only

Seven Pines Lodge *Box 4*
Lewis, WI 54851
715-653-2323

Owners/Operators:
Joan and David Simpson

Guests at this country inn will be surprised such a secluded forest hideaway is so close to the Twin Cities (85 miles). This is the fishing retreat of Charles Lewis, a Minneapolis man who owned a stock brokerage and grain exchange. Lewis bought 1530 acres from a St. Croix steamboat operator threatening to sell the virgin white pine to loggers. Lewis had been coming to fish the little trout stream and he loved the pines.

In the winter of 1903, he turned a few acres into a magnificent log estate: a main lodge, a stream house, an office by the gate (complete with a tickertape machine so he could do business), a garage and a glass-roofed swimming pool of hand-laid tiles, two dairy farms and several trout ponds. All are still there except the dairies and pool house.

Lewis' wife sold it after his death in 1932. Now, several owners later, it's owned by Joan and David Simpson, but Lewis would still feel at home. Many original furnishings remain. One reason the lodge is on the National Register of Historic Places is because President Calvin Coolidge stayed there. The other is its architecture. Huge screened porches, solid log beams, a log stairway, a giant fireplace and wainscotting ceilings make it cozy. The stream house has a porch around all four sides, like a top-heavy fort.

Today, fishermen buy memberships to fish year 'round (there's no license or limit on the private, stocked stream). Overnight guests can fish for $15 extra, then must join to fish again. But they can order trout for dinner (or breakfast). The lodge only is open in the winter for groups of 10 or more to x-c ski. Groups rent it for retreats, weddings and mystery weekends. Rascal, the cat, will spend a night in a guestroom.

Rooms and Rates: Five in Main Lodge, ranging from $54.95 -$67.95; some share bath, extra shower room available, twins and doubles. Also gate ($74.95) and stream ($67.95) houses open in summer. Rates include continental breakfast. Add tax.

Trout was excellent!

54

Meals: Continental breakfast included; three meals by reservation. Joan cooks a selection of two or three dinners. Expect homemade breads, jams. Meals open to public by reservation.

Dates open: Year 'round; winter for groups of 10 or more only

Smoking: Not in rooms   **Children:** Yes   **Pets:** No

Nearby: X-c skiing on 10 miles of trails and trout fishing out the door; close to canoe rentals, hot air balloon rides, sugar bushes, cheese factories, pottery, art and antique shops, Crex Meadows Wildlife Refuge on the St. Croix River.

Directions from Twin Cities: Sent upon reservation. Basically, I-35 north to Highway 8 east to Highway 35 north through Frederic to Lewis.

Deposit: First night's lodging (note: reservations are required)

Payment: Cash, personal or traveler's checks only

The Lowell House B&B Inn

531 Wood
Old Frontenac, MN 55026
612-345-2111

Owner/Operator:
  Barbara Lowell

Barb and Tom Lowell's Greek Revival home in Old Frontenac was built in 1856 as the Schneider boarding house, general store and tavern. It was one of the first buildings in the tiny village, which was founded in the 1850s by New York and Kentucky families as a hunting and fishing retreat above Lake Pepin, part of the Mississippi River.

Barb and Tom, both artists, had been restoring homes in the St. Paul area and bought this historic home in December 1976. "It had been empty for a couple of years and in an estate," said Barb. "It had no indoor plumbing and it was moving off the foundation." Only basic electricity had been installed.

Four years later, the house had all new plumbing and wiring and is otherwise modernized inside. Barb opened the B&B in July 1982, open mostly summers only because she and Tom often go to Mexico to paint during the winters. Guests have use of the dining room and an information/sitting room upstairs. Breakfast is in the dining room.

The house is on the National Register of Historic Places, and the village in which it sits is a gem, as well. Old Frontenac has some glorious mansions remaining, as well as the cottages in which the construction workers lived. The village's blocks are divided by one-lane gravel roads, just right for an evening stroll or bike ride.

"It's so quiet here," Barb said, "it usually takes people a while to wind down from the cities." Miles of Frontenac State Park trails nearby and the possibility of seeing the village via a buggy ride ease the transition.

Rooms and Rates: Four - One with private bath with shower, brown carpet and blue iron double bed - $55 double. Other three share a bath with tub - $45 double. Amy's Room is bright with floral paper and a double bed. Stencil Room has an antique double bed with hand-stenciled walls. Other room with two twin beds is antique furnished. Add tax.

Meals: Breakfast only, usually cheese, fresh fruits, homemade pecan rolls, coffee, tea and orange juice. Other meals available within 10 minutes driving distance.

Dates open: May through October, possibly in other months - call ahead.

Smoking: Yes, but with respect to other guests and not at breakfast.

Children: 13 and older   **Pets:** No

Nearby: Historic neighborhood homes from the 1850-60s. Frontenac State Park trails and bird sanctuary within walking distance. View of Wisconsin from bluffs above Lake Pepin, 3 blocks. Antique shops in short drive.

Directions from Twin Cities: Highway 61 south, 10 miles past Red Wing to County Road 2, turn left. Pass state park, go 3 blocks past church on right side, turn left. Lowell House is tan with shutters, on the left.

Deposit: Full amount

Payment: Cash, personal or traveler's checks only

[handwritten notes in top margin: approx. 46 yr old. student at Dakota ? v? teck in Int? "Have a sailboat" kids "Prime interest" Part owner of mortgage co. ??]

The Rahilly House

304 S. Oak Street
Lake City, MN 55041
612-345-4664

Owners:
Dorene and Gary Fechtmeyer
Innkeepers:
Denise and Mark Peters

John Stout built this house in 1862 for his sister, Eliza and her husband, Harvey Williamson, Lake City's first postmaster. Since then, owners included: in 1882, Morris Russell, Lake City's first newspaper publisher; in 1883, Melissa Buck and her daughter for the town's first clothing store; in 1901, Patrick Rahilly, state senator and Irish immigrant; in 1932, Rahilly's son-in-law, McCahill; in 1963, George Enz, Ziegfeld Follies singer.

The vacant classic Greek revival home was purchased in 1983 by Dorene And Gary Fechtmeyer. Having had two fires and badly in need of repair, the huge home required new plumbing, wiring and roofing. A commercial kitchen was installed, and, after major redecorating, the B&B opened in June 1984. Guests can look at a photo album showing the restoration.

Guests have use of the screened porch, upstairs sundeck, parlor, dining room and living room, which can also be transferred into a guest room. An antique victrola can be played. A social hour with hors d'oeuvres is at 5:30 after 5 p.m. check-in. Breakfast is served family-style.

The quilts and antiques are for sale. Small business groups can be accommodated.

Rooms and Rates: Seven - Six sleep two in double beds; one with private bath, other six share three baths. Doughty Room used to be the dining room, and has original antique buffet and window seats - $80. Williamson Room has pocket doors which can be pulled shut and two double-bed couches; a huge bath off the dining room is used - $60 double. Other rooms are upstairs, examples include: Russell Room has working fireplace, is done in beiges - $70. Buck Room, also in beiges, has antique brass bed - $60. Rahilly Room is dark green and rose, has a sink - $80. Add tax. *"Enz" fireplace shared bath.*

STAYED IN RUSSELL ROOM 1/15/88

58

Meals: Breakfast is at 9 a.m. and includes freshly ground coffee, juice, homemade pastries or breads, fresh fruit in season, plus a varied entree, such as seafood quiche or Tahitian French Toast. Dinner and lunch may be arranged for groups.

Dates open: Year 'round

Smoking: Not in guest rooms

Children: 13 and older

Pets: No

Nearby: Largest marina on Mississippi, two blocks. Downtown shops, two blocks. Day and dinner river cruises, antique shopping. Downhill and x-c skiing within a few minutes. Canoe Zumbro River. Bikes for guests' use; horse-drawn hay rides.

Directions from Twin Cities: Highway 61 south to Lake City. Turn right on Marion Street (one block before the YMCA), go two blocks. House on corner of Oak and Marion.

Deposit: $25

Payment: Cash, personal or traveler's checks only

Great River Farm

General Delivery
Stockholm, WI 54769
715-442-5656

Owner/Operator:
Leland P. Krebs, Jr.

The Peterson family founded Stockholm, which overlooks the Mississippi River's Lake Pepin, in 1854, and brother Jacob built this stone house on the southern edge of town in 1869. Three generations of Petersons lived on the farm until Leland Krebs bought it in 1980.

Krebs, who lived in St. Paul and then Florida, "came back specifically to sheep farm. I was just acting on a dream of mine to have a small farm," he said. For four years, until 1984, he actively farmed the 45 acres, then reached a point with the economics of the business where he had to expand or leave sheep farming. He chose not to expand, and opened a B&B in late 1984 after rewiring, replumbing, scraping and painting. "I wanted a way to make the property productive in some way." Soybeans now cover 20 acres, and guests are free to roam over the land.

Structurally, no changes had been made in the house. The first floor is built into the hillside. Heated by wood, guests can sit around the parlor woodstove. Blair & Ketchum's "Country Journal" sits alongside the binoculars for viewing the migratory birds using the Mississippi flyway.

"Guests have pretty much the feel of visiting a friend here," Krebs said. "It's a restful, scenic and serene environment." Some come specifically to eat at the renowned Harbor View Cafe in Pepin, where Krebs works as a bartender; he checks people in, shows them around and then they have the place to themselves. Breakfast is whenever guests like, sometimes served on the porch, and Krebs is available all morning.

Rooms and Rates: Three - two with double beds, one $45, other one a larger room with huge wooden bed and working woodstove - $55; third room done in blue with twin beds - $45. Singles $5 less; no extra person. All share bath with tub and shower; all have down comforters, original wood floors, family antiques and period pieces. Two rooms at a time are available; Krebs lives in the third.

Meals: Breakfast is served at guests' leisure and may include fresh fruit, fresh eggs, French toast, waffles; homemade muffins, gingerbread or coffeecake; fresh ground coffee.

Dates open: April 15 through November

Smoking: On porch only

Children: Depends - check with owner

Pets: No

Nearby: Lake Pepin on Mississippi and Stockholm, 2 blocks, with art gallery with local artists, country store, rare and used book shop, and Amish country store. Marina and restaurant in Pepin, 6 miles. Birdwatching, sailing, hiking, bicycling.

Directions from Twin Cities: Highway 61 south to near Hastings, turn off to Prescott, Wis. Then Co. Rd. Q and then Co. Rd. E to Highway 35 along Mississippi to farm with the red barn and buildings at south edge of Stockholm.

Deposit: $20 per night reserved

Payment: Cash, personal or traveler's checks only

The Anderson House

333 N. Main
Wabasha, MN 55981
612-565-4524
Minn. toll-free 1-800-862-9702

Owners/Innkeepers:
Jeanne Hall and son John Hall

Listed on the National Register of Historic Places, this is Minnesota's oldest operating hotel. Service has never ceased since opening in 1856, and many of the original fixtures remain. So does the family ownership, now in its fourth generation. Grandma Anderson's cooking, learned in the Pennsylvania Dutch Amish country, remains a mainstay of the hotel.

The hotel has received national publicity for its "cat house" offer - guests can have a cat assigned to them during the stay, and it will be brought to their room sometime in the early evening for the overnight. The idea is a big hit with cat lovers who had to leave Puff home. Another service is a holdover from earlier days: order up some hot bricks for the foot of the bed.

Guest rooms are upstairs from two large dining rooms. Being more than 130 years old, the squeaky floors, doors that don't shut exactly tight, hallway floors that aren't quite level, and baths down the hall seem appropriate. There are no elevators or bellboys, and there's no extra charge for television in the room.

Downstairs, an apartment has been redone into a 200-seat dining room. The room's Pennsylvania Dutch wallpaper emphasizes the traditions carried on in the kitchen. Business groups can be accommodated here. A screened porch and another dining room also are available. A bakery sells take-home treats.

Rooms and Rates: 42 - Rooms are done in bright and light blues, greens, pinks and reds; some original furniture remains. The Bridal Suite has green carpet; white, pink and green wallpaper; marble-top furniture and private bath. The Mayo Suite occupies the turret and is done in red and white. $29.50 - $50 for single and double rooms, $65.50 - $69 for suites. Add tax. Packages available.

Meals: Three meals a day available in ground floor dining rooms, plus bakery. On Sunday, dinner only served 11:30 a.m. - 8 p.m.

Dates open: Year 'round   **Smoking:** Yes

Children: Yes   **Pets:** Yes; "house cats" available

Nearby: Downtown, 2 blocks. Mississippi River, 1 block. Country roads, antique shopping, fishing, boating.

Directions from Twin Cities: Highway 61 south to Wabasha, easy to find on Main Street.

Deposit: $25

Payment: Cash, personal or traveler's checks only

Gallery House

215 N. Main
Alma, WI 54610
608-685-4975

Owners/Operators:
Joan and John Runions

This three-room B&B is located in an historic mercantile building whose first floor has served Alma since 1861 as restaurants, a hardware store, post office, library, floor covering store, antique shops and dentist offices.

Jacob Iberg had the building constructed for a store and home. Peter Polin and John Tester leased and then owned the building from the 1860s, operating a general store that did an excellent business as Alma grew as a grain depot. The Polin family remained owners until 1913.

Today, the building is on the National Register of Historic Places. John Runions' watercolor studio is located there along with a gallery. Joan Runions operates the Gallery Spice Shoppe on the other side of the gallery. Runions moved in 1974 from Chicago with two of their four children for John's business.

"The scenery is the biggest thing," he said. "The material is here." When they drove through Alma and the area, "Lake Pepin just rang bells." The store was empty then, and the family lived upstairs. After the youngest children moved out, "we had all this space," Joan says. They opened the B&B in June 1985, after replumbing, rewiring and redecorating.

The B&B is upstairs in what used to be, at various times, a boarding house and apartments. Guests enter the long hall from the back, and they have access to the Runions living and dining rooms at the end of the hall. The three rooms are off the hall and share a bath. A deck goes around the side of the building for guests.

Rooms and Rates: Three - All doubles, share bath with clawfoot tub and shower. One has a sink in the room and all are done in yellow and gold; brass bed in #3, antique wood bed in #2. $35 per room. Add tax.

Meals: Breakfast is at 8 a.m. (so the shops can open at 9) and includes juice, coffee and tea; fresh fruit plate or compote; homemade raisin bran muffins; cheese and sausage fritatta, pancakes or French toast; bacon.

Dates open: Year 'round   **Smoking:** No

Children: No   **Pets:** No

Nearby: Country roads for fall colors; river fishing. Lock and dam, 1 block. Trail up to Buena Vista Park, overlooks Mississippi, in back of house. Swimming beach, canoe rental, tennis court, marina with boat rental, 1 mile. Golf, 8 miles south.

Directions from Twin Cities: Highway 61 south to Wabasha, cross river, turn right at Nelson. Alma is nine miles away.

Deposit: First night's lodging

Payment: Cash, personal or traveler's checks, VISA or MasterCard

The Laue House

1111 S. Main
Alma, WI 54610
608-685-4923

Owners/Operators:
Jan and Jerry Schreiber

Jan and Jerry Schreiber, who are natives of nearby Nelson, Wis., and Alma, respectively, are retired and enjoy restoring historic buildings. The Laue House was built in 1863 by successful sawmill owner Fred Laue, a German immigrant who moved to Alma after living in Cincinnati. It is on the National Register of Historic Places.

When the Schreibers bought the single-family home overlooking the Mississippi in 1977, only three rooms on the first floor were being used. It had no eaves, light fixtures or furniture, and the porch was falling off. Schreibers found the original architectural drawings in the attic, from which they had decorative wrought iron and 27 wooden brackets replicated.

"My original intention was to save this domestic Italianate structure, being as it's the only one in Alma," said Jerry. But when a power plant was constructed nearby and workers wanted to rent rooms, the idea for a B&B was conceived.

This place is spartan and casual. If Jan and Jerry aren't in, guests check themselves in and pick an empty room. Likewise, breakfast is toast-your-own English muffin. Guests may use the player piano downstairs and a refrigerator. Don't expect little individual bars of soap and matching towels; guests share a bar of soap just like at home, the upstairs bathroom shower stall is utilitarian, and rooms are not carpeted.

Schreibers will take guests on parties on river sandbars, and guests can clean fish or cook out in the back. The front porch is a favorite spot to sit and watch the river go by. Trains speed by and rattle the windows.

Rooms and Rates: Five upstairs - The large white room overlooks the river, has two double beds, plus a small color cable TV and a sink - $16 single, $26 . The other rooms have B&W cable TV - $14 single, $22 double. All share a bath with a shower. A tub is available downstairs. Add tax.

Meals: Breakfast is serve-yourself English muffin, grape jelly and coffee.

Dates open: Usually closed January - March, but call ahead.

Smoking: Yes   **Children:** "Small families are OK"

Pets: "We love pets if they're well-behaved." Schreibers have a dog.

Nearby: Country roads for fall colors; river fishing. Lock and dam within walking distance. Boat rental across the highway. Free boat launching.

Directions from Twin Cities: Highway 61 south to Wabasha, cross river, turn right at Nelson, Wis. Alma is nine miles away; Laue House is last one on south side of town, near power plant.

Deposit: Not necessary

Payment: Cash, personal or traveler's checks only

Canterbury Inn B&B

723 Second St. SW
Rochester, MN 55902
507-289-5553

Owners/Operators:
Mary Martin and
Jeffrey Van Sant

For Mary Martin and Jeffrey Van Sant, opening a B&B was more a question of where than when or how. The two women met in St. Louis and became good friends while getting divorced. Jeffrey was a church administrator and Mary was a nurse. "We both like to take care of people," Jeffrey said. "Besides, we had the same china pattern," she adds with a laugh.

One of the problems, though, was that most towns that depend on tourism in this part of the country have only seasonal lodgings. They checked into locations as far away as the Caribbean. On one trip to Rochester, they realized that people coming to the Mayo Clinic and IBM, for instance, would mean year 'round business. The Rochester realtor they called had been hoping someone would do a B&B there and had a property in mind.

The house for sale was used as a French restaurant, Broadstreet Cafe, that had outgrown itself. Dairyman Samuel Hall had built the home in 1890, and it remained in his family until the mid 1970s. The restaurant owners were the first owners outside the family. "Nobody ever chopped up the house or painted or did anything funny to it," Mary said. They bought it, put in new bathrooms and redecorated, then opened in April 1983.

Guests are treated to "tea" from 5:30 to 7 with wine and baked brie, pate or other hors d'oeuvres. They may use the living and dining rooms downstairs. Martin and Van Sant include special touches, like blanket covers on the beds and a willingness to drive guests to appointments or provide flexible breakfast times.

Rooms and Rates: Four - All have private bath with shower and tub, and are decorated with family period pieces and done with natural wood. Bed sizes in the four rooms are queen, king, two twins, and either a king or two twins. $55 singles; $65 doubles. Add tax.

Meals: Breakfast is served any time in the dining room or guest rooms, and includes juices, coffee and tea; homemade breads; Norwegian fruit soup, baked apples or fresh fruit; and an entree such as Grand Marnier French toast, baked German apple pancakes, wild rice waffles, pesto omelettes or eggs benedict. ("Tea" may suffice as evening meal.)

Dates open: Year 'round

Smoking: First floor only

Children: "By consultation"

Pets: No

Nearby: Mayo Clinic and St. Mary's Hospital, 3 blocks; antiques, restaurants, shops, theaters, symphony, jewelry and art galleries, 4-6 blocks; Mayowood, about 5 miles; x-c skiing, golf, 10 miles; canoeing Zumbro River, 30 miles.

Directions from Twin Cities: Highway 52 south, exit on Second St. SW, turn left and about nine blocks.

Deposit: First night's lodging or confirmed by credit card

Payment: Cash, personal or traveler's checks, VISA, MasterCard or AMEX

Grand Old Mansion

501 Clay St.
Mantorville, MN 55955
507-635-3231

Owners/Operators:
Irene and Clair Felker

This 10-room mansion on a hill overlooking Mantorville was built in 1899 for Teunis Slingerland, a wealthy landowner. At the time, he spent $5,000 for it. The Slingerlands lived there until 1939. Their estate was then sold for $500 in back taxes to Walter Stussy, who did not want to see it torn down. Stussy was a Mantorville farmer who spent most of his professional life touting the values of the local limestone.

Not wanting to appear too pretentious, it took Walter and Esther Stussy until 1942 to move into their home. Irene, their daughter, adapted more quickly, having admired the house since her childhood.

Today, Irene Stussy Pappas Felker and Clair Felker, her husband, run the home as a living museum. It is full of antiques, art and dark wood. The house is open for tours, and tour groups are not uncommon.

Irene, in addition to operating the B&B and house tours, runs a beauty shop in an attached building, acts as a tour guide for Mantorville, and collects china bells, plates, cats and other figurines.

Three rooms are rented on the second floor, and sometimes the Felker's bedroom is available. It has a round, bright red bed draped by a red lace canopy.

Guests have free use of a third-floor lounge, with modern decor and barnwood-like paneling. It has a TV and an electric fireplace.

Rooms and Rates: Three rooms: The Green Room has a king-sized bed with a blue spread and a private bath with tub - $35. The Blue Room has two double beds; the Gold Room has an antique double bed; they share a bath with tub and shower - $27.50 each. $7.50 per extra person in the Blue Room. Add tax.

Meals: Breakfast is served in one of two dining rooms and includes juice, coffee; French toast, pancakes or bacon and eggs.

Dates open: Year 'round

Smoking: Yes

Children: Yes

Pets: No

Nearby: Antique shops, restaurants, Opera House with melodramas, tennis, park by river, 1-3 blocks; limestone quarry, 1.5 miles; golf, 2 miles.

Directions from Twin Cities: Highway 52 to Hader; turn right/south on Highway 57 at Hader, about 25 miles to Mantorville. Turn right on Fifth Street, 1 block to Clay.

Deposit: $10 per room per night

Payment: Cash, personal or traveler's checks

The American House

410 E. Third St.
Morris, MN 56267
612-589-4054

Owners/Operators:
   Karen and Kyle Berget

"I'd always driven by when I moved out here five years ago and thought, 'What a neat house.' It reminded me of Stillwater and I was homesick for it," said Karen Berget, a native of Stillwater, the St. Croix River town replete with turn-of-the-century mansions. She's stayed in the B&Bs there and spent her wedding night at the Lowell Inn, so it wasn't surprising when she and Kyle toured this Victorian home and thought it would make a good B&B.

Built in 1901, the house had 11 owners before the Bergets, one of whom was a wealthy judge and farmer who moved into town for the winter so his children could attend school. The home was cut up into a duplex in the 1940s, and remained that way until Bergets bought it in May 1984.

Starting, literally, from the ground up, they moved some walls, replastered, and did other major renovation. The restoration, which took six months, was not without its surprises, the best of which was in the dining room. Hidden under carpeting was a walnut and oak parquet floor known as a "picture frame" floor because of its design of walnut borders. The dining room also had original handstenciled wall borders, and Karen added her own in guest rooms.

A study in the local historical society records provided the name for the B&B, taken from the first hotel in Morris, built in 1875. Guests can use the dining room, a toy room upstairs with TV and games, and "we have a bicycle built for two that we encourage guests to tour Morris on." Also, luncheons are served to small groups.

Rooms and Rates: Three - All double beds, furnished with antiques and quilts; all share bath with clawfoot tub, no shower. Anna's Room, which used to be the kitchen in the upstairs apartment, has partial canopy bedroom set from old Curtis Hotel, Mpls. - $30. Elizabeth's Room is in blue and white with handstenciled walls - $30. Christian John's Room has two matching antique beds, sleeps up to four - $35. Tax included.

Meals: Breakfast is served in the dining room at a time convenient for guests and includes juice, milk, non-alcoholic amaretto coffee; omelettes, buttermilk pancakes, sausage, or bacon; rolls or coffee cake; fresh fruit.

Dates open: Year 'round

Smoking: Designated areas

Children: Yes

Pets: No

Nearby: University of Minnesota-Morris, 2 blocks; bike path to city park, 4 blocks; city park with swimming, 1 mile; downtown shops, restaurants, 6 blocks.

Directions from Twin Cities: I-94 northwest to Sauk Centre exit, west on Highway 28 to Morris; left on Atlantic Ave. (main street) through stop lights to Third St., left on Third to corner of Columbia Ave.

Deposit: Half of room rate

Payment: Cash, personal or traveler's checks only

Deposit $35

CK in 3pm / CK out by noon

Dec 12

Within 3 hours

Mrs. B's Historic Lanesboro Inn

101 Parkway
Lanesboro, MN 55949
507-467-2154

Owners/Operators:
Nancy and Jack Bratrud
and family

The Bratruds fell in love with Lanesboro and bought 100 acres in 1980. Jack and Nancy later bought an old building in downtown Lanesboro, pretty much on a whim. When the city wanted to keep that building for a museum and offered them "a much better building" across the street, they agreed. "We became more and more serious about leaving Minneapolis," Jack said.

Empty building in hand, they thought about a restaurant or office space. But the design that looked ideal was a country inn. The building, now on the National Register of Historic Places, was constructed in 1872 of local limestone from the cliffs in the Root River valley. "It had three owners," Nancy says, "the Thompson and Thompson brothers, the Thompson and Thompson brothers, and the Johnsons." The Thompsons weren't related, but all owners operated a combination furniture store/mortuary in the building.

Everything but the wood flooring was rebuilt, plumbing was installed for the first time, and the stone exterior was restored. "Our concept was to give guests a little more privacy," Nancy said, pointing to soundproofed walls. The lobby has a baby grand piano, and guests can use decks on side of the building. Guests receive complimentary sherry and chocolate kisses. Tea is served about 4 p.m. The restaurant in the basement has a breakfast room, just for guests, and a dining room, often open to the public for lunches and dinners. Menus feature regional foods, perhaps including Root River trout or bread with flour stone-ground at the Stockton mill.

Rooms and Rates: Nine - all queen beds; all private baths, seven have tub, two shower only. Each room is different, but three have canopied, four-poster beds - $40 weekdays, $70 Friday and Saturday. Some have partial canopies; all others $35 weekdays, $65 weekends. Other examples include #9, with a Norwegian "cupboard bed" requiring a small step-stool to reach; #3 is done in rose and grey, has rocking chairs on the deck. $8 per additional person in room. Add tax.

→ 5 course meal $19.95/person 2½ hr

8-9

Meals: Breakfast is included in room rate and may include wild blackberries, local sausage, fresh eggs, seven-grain pancakes and homemade breads. Lunches and dinners seasonally, Wed. - Sun., and for groups.

Dates open: Year 'round   **Smoking:** Designated areas only

Children: "Not ideal but not prohibited." No toddlers

Pets: $100 cash deposit plus inspection; kept in kennel cases on outdoor decks adjacent to guest rooms

Nearby: Root River hiking, biking and x-c ski trail, 1/2 block. Museum, woodcarver's shop and winery, 1 block. Guided cave tours, fishing, hunting canoeing, golf and tennis.

Directions from Twin Cities: Highways 52/55 south to Rochester, then 52 south to Fountain. Left out of Fountain on Co. Rd. 8, eight miles to Lanesboro.

Deposit: $30

Payment: Cash, personal or traveler's checks only

85 $95 w fireplace

Carriage House B&B

420 Main St.
Winona, MN 55987
507-452-8256

Owners/Operators:
Debi and Don Salyards

In 1870, Conrad Böhn, a sill and sash manufacturer, owned a whole block of Winona's Main Street. His factory was where a church now stands on the corner. His gigantic home is near the other corner. The three-story carriage house alone housed six carriages and several horses, complete with stable boys' rooms and a hayloft.

Bohn lost the property for back taxes in the 1890s, but it survived several owners, including a dentist who added an office to the side of the house. Deb and Don Salyards bought it in 1977.

When Don, an economics professor and entrepreneur, took a sabbatical and the couple traveled, the idea came to convert the carriage house, which was not being fully used, to a B&B. The Salyards liked staying in B&Bs when they traveled, "and we both like people," said Deb, who is active in the Winona Historical Society.

Complete interior renovation included adding insulation, plumbing, wiring, soundproofed walls and bathrooms, as well as a summer porch. The B&B opened in August 1986 with four second-floor rooms, two of which were the stable boys'. Guests use a private entrance, and have breakfast on the porch or delivered to their rooms. The hallway has a brass hitching post as part of the railing, and a refrigerator and coffee pot are available for guests' use. Complimentary small bottles of wine and soft drinks are included.

Rooms and Rates: Two sharing a bath, plus two-bedroom suite which shares a bath. All double four-poster beds. Pedestal sinks in each room. Baths have shower only. Rooms done in "country" wallpaper and each has its own decor in mauve, blue, beige and off-white, with a resident teddy bear. $25 - $30 double rooms, $50 suite Nov. 1-April 31; $40 and $45 double rooms, $80 suite May 1 - Oct. 31. $7 for third person in room. Add tax.

Meals: Breakfast is delivered to the room at a time guests indicate the night before, and includes fresh fruit, muffins, croissant, sweet rolls, jams, juices and coffee.

Dates open: Year 'round   **Smoking:** On porch only

Children: 12 and older   **Pets:** No

Nearby: Lake Winona and bike trails, 4 blocks; Mississippi River and levee park, 4 blocks; Armory Museum, 5 blocks; community theather and Winona State University, 1 block; antique and craft stores, restaurants, 3 blocks.

Directions from Twin Cities: Highway 61 south to Winona, left on Highway 43, follow 43, which turns into Main Street.

Deposit: $25

Payment: Cash, personal or traveler's checks only

The Hotel

129 W. Third St.   Owner: David Nudd
Winona, MN 55987   Managers: Sandy and Ted Jafvert
507-452-5460

When it opened Oct. 1, 1982, the Schlitz Hotel was called "an ornament to the city" by the Winona Daily Republican. Costing $36,000, the three-story, Milwaukee cream brick hotel was "a piece of architectural work and substantiability for which this company is noted," the newspaper said, referring to the builders, Schlitz Brewing Co., of Milwaukee. A classy traveling man's hotel where women were not welcome, the paper reported a cigar salesroom and bar were on the ground floor with the dining room.

Somewhere within the next 55 or so years, the hotel did a flip-flop, turning into a virtual flophouse with $8 a night rooms. The Williams Hotel, as it was later known, was rumored to break occupancy records of sorts, renting one room 10 times in one night. David Nudd, of LaCrosse, wanted to give The Hotel a new beginning at again being "an ornament" to Winona when he bought it in 1980 with a partner.

Restoration is most visible in the lobbies and stairways. The original backdrop from a local opera house hangs on the third floor landing. (The Chrysler advertisement on it was innovative at the time because it shows a woman driving.) The oak banisters are originals, and the original hotel desk can be seen now as second floor office. Also visible is an unusual interior brick wall. If ghosts interest you, check in to room #19, where a light appears early in the mornings and the door sometimes open mysteriously.

On the ground floor, Theo's serves liquor and food and has video games.

Rooms and Rates: 25 - All modernized with private baths (some with showers only), color TVs, phones and large window air conditioners. No original furnishings were left, so reproductions decorate the suites, such as the Princess Winona Suite, with a settee and marble top tables. $24.95 to $38.50 singles, $33 to $48.50 doubles, suites $74.50. Add tax.

Meals: Three meals available on ground-floor restaurant, Theo's, plus saloon with original wood floor. Banquet facilities.

Dates open: Year 'round

Smoking: Yes

Children: Yes

Pets: No

Nearby: Winona County Historical Society Museum, 1 block. Riverfront park and riverboat excursions and dinner cruises, 3 blocks. Historic home tours; Polish Heritage Museum.

Directions from Twin Cities: Highway 61 south to Winona. Hotel located at the corner of Third and Johnson streets, downtown.

Deposit: Confirmed by credit card number

Payment: Cash, personal or traveler's checks, VISA or MasterCard

The Mansion

3600 London Rd.   Owners/Operators:
Duluth, MN 55804   Sue and Warren Monson and family
218-724-0739

Nobody can say the Monsons haved named their B&B inaccurately. This is the spectacular estate of Harry Dudley, a mining engineer who did international business, and Marjorie Congdon Dudley, one of the six Congdon children born and raised at Glensheen mansion, just a half mile away.

Marjorie and Harry were married in 1918. In 1930, Harry brought her back to the neighborhood of her childhood, to live in a home that reportedly cost $100,000 at the time, excluding land and other buildings. The Dudleys raised two boys in the home, which had 13 bedrooms, 10 of which were for staff or guests.

In 1982, the Monsons found the mansion while looking for land on Lake Superior. "We fell in love with it and had to have a reason to swing it," says Sue Monson. The "reason" was a B&B she and three children would run in the summers while Warren, a doctor, would keep his practice in Browerville. As the first B&B in Duluth, city officials allow operation only six months a year. Before opening in May 1983, the house needed to be completely furnished and outfitted. The next big projects were reinsulating, after getting a first-year utility bill as big as some people's mortgages, and replacing 75 missing storm windows out of 300 total. Warren has since moved his practice to West Duluth.

Guests may use the six acres of grounds, 525 feet of shoreline, a huge screened porch, living room, dining room, library and first floor bathroom.

Rooms and Rates: Nine - All rooms have queen or king beds. Four are former servants' rooms, so they're smallest. The Houseman's Room has private bath, is on first floor - $85. The Yellow, Peach and Beige rooms share two baths - $65 each. Pink Room has antiques, a china tub - $95. Green and Blue rooms share interconnecting bathroom and face lake - $95 each. The South Guest Room is a huge lakeside room, also with china tub - $130. The Anniversary Suite is only room on the third floor, with lake view, private bath - $130. Add tax. Add $25 per extra person over two.

Meals: Breakfast is from 8:30 - 9:30 a.m. in the dining room and includes five kinds of juice, beverages, bacon and eggs, toast or muffins, danish or caramel rolls.

Dates open: Memorial Day to Oct. 15, plus winter weekends

Children: Depends on circumstances - check with owner

Smoking: Not in guest rooms   **Pets:** No

Nearby: Glensheen Mansion, a few blocks; 10 minutes to downtown Duluth

Directions from Twin Cities: I-35 to Duluth, follow signs for Highway 61/North Shore Drive, look for 3600 signs on right past Glensheen.

Deposit: $50 on six large rooms; $25 on three smaller rooms

Payment: Cash, personal or traveler's checks, VISA or MasterCard

Fitger's Inn

600 E. Superior St.
Duluth, MN 55802
218-722-8826 (call collect)

Owner:
    Fitger's Inn Limited Partnership
Operator: Historic Inns of America
General Manager: Vickie Pirkola

Fitger's Inn opened in November 1984 in a series of historic buildings, listed on the National Register of Historic Places. The 10-building complex had been constructed over the years as a brewery in downtown Duluth. When the last beer was bottled in 1972, Fitger Brewing Company, the last of a long list of brewery owners, closed its doors on Duluth's longest running business. When the buildings opened again, they were a 48-room hotel, restaurant, large shopping mall and parking lot overlooking Lake Superior.

Sidney Luce was the first to try brewing in Duluth, which he intended as an economic stimulant during an 1857 depression. In 1882, another owner hired German immigrant August Fitger, a German brew school graduate. Within two years, Fitger owned half the company.

Fitger beer was more in demand than ever as the Iron Range's miners thirsted. Prohibition didn't stop success - pop, "near beer" and cigars were sold. Just before World War II, 100,000 barrels of Fitger beer were produced a year.

The hotel itself has been built in the former bottling plant. The loading dock's beams can still be seen out the windows on the second level, lake side. The original tellers cage and safe are in the lobby; the hotel lobby was the shipping and receiving office. In many rooms, the massive exterior rock walls have been left uncovered. A self-guided walking tour of the complex is offered. Parking ramp is free (it used to be the barn for beer wagon horses).

Rooms and Rates: 48 - All with tub and shower and queen or king-sized beds. Thick carpeting, antique reproductions and turn-of-the-century decor, perhaps with two or four-poster beds. Rates range from $58.95 for a single, street-side, to $260 for the Lake Superior Suite, a room the size of three with a four-poster bed and single whirlpool. Most rates in the $60-80 range. Lakeside rooms $5 more. Add tax. Seasonal corporate rates; banquet and meeting facilities.

$129   64.50
    $69.95 *Street*
    79.95

Meals: Three meals available in Fitger's Restaurant in the complex; other restaurants also open in the mall.

Dates open: Year 'round   **Smoking:** Yes

Children: Yes   **Pets:** No

Nearby: Shopping and dining in mall complex; outdoor patio by lake. Shops springing up along Superior Street; many shops within walking distance.

Directions from Twin Cities: I-35 to Duluth, follow Superior Street to Fitger's, on the right.

Deposit: First night's lodging

Payment: Cash, traveler's checks, VISA, MasterCard or AMEX

Rosenberry Inn

511 Franklin
Wausau, WI 54401
715-842-5733

Owners/Operators:
Patty and Jerry Artz
and son Doug Artz

When Patty and Jerry Artz looked for an historic home in Wausau to remodel into a B&B, they had their sights set on a white Victorian mansion on Franklin Street. But when they discovered it had few rooms and plenty of work, they looked at a property just down the street they didn't think they'd consider. The green stucco home was "prairie school" architecture - clean lines, nothing full of gingerbread or other decoration. "It was modernized paneling and drop ceilings," cut into eight tiny studio apartments back in the '40s and not very attractive.

But the eight rooms already had bathrooms and kitchenettes, a plus for a B&B. They liked the woodwork that remained. When they bought the home in January 1985, it was part of the 61-property Andrew Warren Historic District and listed on the National Register of Historic Places. The Artz's were determined to restore it to a condition of which its original owner would have been proud.

That owner was Marvin Rosenberry, a chief justice of the Wisconsin Supreme Court for 21 years, and Kate, his wife. The house was built in 1908, during Wausau's lumber boom, when neighbors were lumber barons and merchants.

The Artz's turned the third floor into their apartment and guest lounge, where guests eat breakfast. The Wisconsin antiques they've collected for years decorate the guest rooms. Restoration included removing four to five coats of wallpaper and paint, indoor-outdoor carpeting, drop ceilings, modern paneling and replacing showers and tubs. Original stained glass windows and doors remain. A huge porch with swing is available for guests.

Rooms and Rates: Eight - All with private bath (some with shower only), kitchenettes, hardwood floors with rag rugs; working fireplaces in rooms 1,2, 5 and 6. Examples include: Room 1 was the library, has a built in bookcase, white iron double bed. Room 4 has a double bed, plus two twin beds on a sunporch, and a window seat. Room 7 is two twins with mallards on the wallpaper. Room 8 has antique bed, clawfoot tub and shower. $40 single; $45 double; $10 per additional person. Add tax.

Meals: Continental breakfast served in gathering room or guest room; includes juice, coffee, rolls and banana bread; sometimes fruit.

Dates open: Year 'round

Smoking: Yes

Children: Yes

Pets: No

Nearby: Parks, Wisconsin River, theater, shopping mall, antique shops, gift shops, restaurants, 4-6 blocks to downtown; Dells of Eau Claire falls and park, 15 miles; ski hill and x-c ski trails, 4-5 miles. Leigh Yawkey Woodson Art Museum, Historical Society, 2-3 blocks.

Directions from Twin Cities: I-94 east to Highway 29E; follow Highway 52 east to Sixth and Franklin.

Deposit: Not necessary

Payment: Cash, personal or traveler's checks, VISA or MasterCard

The Naniboujou Lodge

Star Route 1, Box 505
Grand Marais, MN 55604
218-387-2688

Owners/Operators:
Nancy and Tim Ramey

In 1928, a group of Duluth businessmen opened the Naniboujou Lodge, 15 miles north of Grand Marais. The mile of Lake Superior shore and 3,300 acres of prime land were designed for riding stables, tennis courts, fishing and hunting. Membership was by invitation "for those of standing," and included Babe Ruth and Jack Dempsey.

But the first members who came by bus or the steamship *America* found few developed trails and no tennis courts. After the stock market crashed, the lodge was foreclosed in 1932 and building materials for a third wing confiscated. The dream of a private men's club was gone.

Arthur Roberts then ran an exclusive resort, complete with valet service, but it closed after his death. Luther and Susie Wallace bought the vacant lodge in 1961 and ran it for nearly 20 years, intending to turn it over to their two sons. But Luke and William, then in their 20s, tragically drowned in a 1977 canoeing accident.

Tim Ramey was their friend, and he and Nancy signed on as managers in 1980 when a Christian group bought it from the Wallaces. The Rameys then purchased it in 1985. Tim and friends winterized and paneled one wing and new wiring and plumbing have been installed throughout. A solarium sitting room next to the dining room was added in 1983. "We don't have a liquor license and we don't have alpine slides," Tim said, "so it's more for people who want to get away from it all."

The dining room remains the Cree Indian Sistine of the north, with bright orange, red, green, blue and yellow art work. Naniboujou, the Cree god of the wilderness, is depicted on a wall. The stone fireplace at one end, with 200 tons of lake rocks in Cree designs, is said to be the largest in the state. The original paintings, hooped curtains and chandeliers remain. The building is on the National Register of Historic Places.

Meals: Three meals a day available in dining room restaurant May through October. Winter meals for groups only.

Rooms and Rates: 29 - Variety of queens, doubles and twin beds in rooms and connecting suites; private baths or communal bath with showers. Winterized wing has knotty pine paneling. Summer wing has Cree design carried into rooms in subdued decoration. Singles - $29 shared bath, $40 private; doubles range from $34 shared bath to $55 for fireplace and private bath. Add tax.

Dates open: May through October. From November, open to groups for conferences, seminars, business meetings, etc.

Smoking: Yes   **Children:** Yes   **Pets:** Discouraged

Nearby: Swimming in Brule River and Lake Superior beaches.
Fishing, hunting, x-c and downhill skiing. Judge Magney State Park across the highway for hiking trails and to see Devil's Kettle in the Brule River.

Directions from Twin Cities: 15 miles north of Grand Marais on Highway 61.

Deposit: First night's lodging

Payment: Cash, personal or traveler's checks, VISA, MasterCard or Diners Club

Young's Island B&B

Gunflint Trail 67-1
Grand Marais, MN 55604
218-388-4688
Minn. toll-free 1-800-622-3583
Out-of-state 1-800-328-3325

Owners/Operators:
Barbara and Ted Young

Those unfortunates without relatives who own a log cabin on an island in a lake off the Gunflint Trail now have the next best thing: Barbara and Ted Young. (If the family squabbles, it's better than next best.)

Located on a sizeable island in Poplar Lake, about 32 miles up the Gunflint Trail from Grand Marais, the B&B is open year 'round. The log cabin was built in the early 1930s as a summer home for a member of a Minneapolis symphony who had meals catered by a nearby lodge and canoed in. The Young family acquired the property in 1952, and Ted and Barbara moved to the island in 1974.

Barbara or Ted meet B&B guests at the landing on the mainland, then take them across by boat (or ski over in winter). Joey, their 11-year-old, collects fresh eggs for breakfast and will give guests an island tour, complete with introductions to the sled dogs, who stay in dog houses far back on the island. The house is heated with wood and has electricity, but not indoor plumbing; guests use the Young's composting toilet and take a sauna in the cooler months or bathe in the lake in the summer.

Youngs have a sand beach for swimming and a canoe is available for guests' use. Moose and bear are frequently seen in the area and fishing and canoeing on Poplar Lake are popular. Ted runs sled dogs, and he and a partner will let would-be mushers have a go at the controls. They operate Boundary Country Trekking for BWCA trips and participate in the Gunflint Trail's cross country lodge-to-lodge ski-through, during which skiers stay with the Youngs at the B&B or in wood-heated Mongolian yurts as they ski along the Banadad Ski Trail.

Rooms and Rates: One - With a double bed. Extra sleeping quarters can be arranged. $25 single, $50 double. Add tax.

Meals: Breakfast, which includes Ted's Baked Eggs (mushrooms, onions, green pepper, bacon, cheese and nutmeg), homemade cranberry muffins, seasonal fruit and cheese platter, juice and coffee. Other meals available on the Gunflint Trail nearby.

Dates open: Year 'round   **Smoking:** Outside

Children: Yes   **Pets:** No

Nearby: Swimming, fishing, canoeing and hut-to-hut cross-country skiing literally out the front door. Hiking trails, hunting, dog sled rides and mushing, camping, Boundary Waters Canoe Area.

Directions from Twin Cities: Turn left on the Gunflint Trail in Grand Marais. Young's landing is the first road to the left past the Windigo Lodge.

Deposit: Half of room rate

Payment: Cash, personal or traveler's checks only

Worth the drive

Westby House

200 W. State St.
Westby, WI 54667
608-634-4112

Owners/Operators:
Patricia Smith & Partners

Patricia Smith knew exactly what she wanted: to combine her interest in antiques and decorating skills with the restaurant and bookkeeping experience of her friend, daughter and son-in-law by renovating an historic home into a restaurant, shop and guest home.

Smith, Annette and Philip Park and Robert Hektner were all Minneapolis residents who took the plunge together after finding the house they wanted in Westby, Wis. It met their structural and financial specifications, as well as those for being in a small town, yet a certain distance to the Twin Cities and a college town (LaCrosse).

Between October 1984, when Smith moved to Westby from Minneapolis, to July 1985, when the Westby House opened, "20 tons of plaster were taken out," she said. While the original woodwork, lights and stained glass in this Victorian home remain, it needed rewiring, replumbing, and redecorating, new ceilings, new porch pillars and railing, as well as the addition of a commercial kitchen for the first floor restaurant. Getting the original buffet up the stairs to the second floor must have been a sight to see, and Smith vows the giant piece is never coming back down.

Built for Martin Bekkedahl, a Norwegian businessman who owned a bank and lumber business in northern Wisconsin and was the first to plant tobacco in the county, the Westby House had only one other owner since its first use in 1892. Throughout the house, antiques are for sale, as are gifts, wallpapers, lace and quilts. The second floor has space for meetings or a two-room suite in the turret room.

Rooms and Rates: Four - Anniversary Suite has a queen brass bed, fainting couch, private bath with tub - $52. Other rooms share a bath with tub and shower, and a half bath. The Greenbrier Room has two double white iron beds and a sink - $42. The Squire Room has two twin beds - $38. The Country Room has a queen iron bed, quilt, tin ceiling - $42. Add tax.

Meals: Continental breakfast (fruit, homemade muffins) included in room rate. Three meals served in restaurant, open 7:30 a.m. - 9 p.m. daily.

Dates open: Year 'round   **Smoking:** Yes

Children: Yes   **Pets:** No

Nearby: Located in town, just a walk to stores and churches. X-c skiing, 1.5 miles; Amish community, 5 miles; biking, Kickapoo River canoe rental, 8 miles. LaCrosse is 29 miles to the northwest.

Directions from Twin Cities: Highway 61 south through LaCrosse, follow 35 and 61, then 14 and 61 to Westby.

Deposit: 20 percent

Payment: Cash, personal or traveler's check, VISA or MasterCard

The Redstone Inn

504 Bluff
Dubuque, IA 52001   Innkeeper:
319-582-1894   Gail Naughton

In 1894, Elizabeth Cooper married Dan Sullivan. Her father, A.A. Cooper, had arrived in Iowa in 1846 with just two bits to his name. But when Elizabeth married, he was a wealthy man, owning the Cooper Wagon Works, makers of prairie schooners. He also was a very practical man. So, when he built Elizabeth a Victorian mansion for her wedding present, he designed it as a 27-room duplex so it could generate income in case her husband could not.

Ninety years later, 17 Dubuque investors spent nearly $1 million to buy, renovate, furnish and ultimately preserve the last of Cooper's mansions. Cooper's own 35-room residence earlier had been flattened into a parking lot. For years, the Redstone had been either apartments, a bar or vacant. The owners spent more than a year renovating and furnishing the mansion, listed on the National Register of Historic Places.

When the Redstone Inn opened in May 1985, it was a Victorian 15-room inn with conveniences and elegance even Elizabeth Cooper never enjoyed. Mauve, burgundy, green and deep blue, which are in the Redstone's original stained glass windows, are used throughout the inn, as is polished woodwork and period antiques, all collected within 100 miles of Dubuque. Visitors register at an oak reception desk and choose rooms by seeing photos of each. The elaborate parlor is available for use by guests. Provisions are available for business groups.

Rooms and Rates: 15 - No two alike, but all have private baths, color TV, phones and individual thermostats. Two suites have fireplaces and four rooms have whirlpools with heavy robes provided. The huge Bridal Suite ($110) has hand-embroidered bedspread on queen bed, heart-shaped soaps, and, like the Governor's Suite ($110), includes breakfast, champagne, cheese and fruit tray. Doubles - $55 and $65; junior suite, whirlpool - $75; deluxe suite, fireplace, conference table - $90. Add tax. Singles $10 less. Extra person over 12 - $10. Cribs $5. Add tax.

Meals: Continental breakfast and afternoon English Tea, complete with cucumber sandwiches, biscuits and tarts, available in dining room. Private meals catered.

Dates open: Year 'round   **Smoking:** Yes

Children: Yes (cribs available)   **Pets:** No

Nearby: Fourth Street Elevator (189-foot cable car), one block; Five Flags civic center/theater, one block; surrounded by three of Dubuque's historic preservation districts with shops. Paddleboat rides, greyhound racing.

Directions from Twin Cities: Check maps; either follow the Mississippi or go south on I-35 and then east. Inn is easy to find in downtown Dubuque.

Deposit: First night's lodging or confirmation by credit card

Payment: Cash, personal or traveler's checks, VISA, MasterCard or AMEX

The Stout House

11th and Locust
Dubuque, IA 52001
319-582-1894

Innkeepers:
Barbara Kopperud and
Jim Borden

After 17 businesspeople formed the Dubuque Historic Improvement Company to buy Elizabeth Cooper's home and open the Redstone Inn, they decided to do it again. This time, the structure is another red sandstone mansion six blocks away. After renovation, the doors to a five-room B&B opened in May 1986 in the Frank D. Stout house.

Built in 1890-91, the $75,000 home served as a grand place for the president of the Knapp Stout Lumber Company to entertain and raise his five children with Clara, his wife. In 1901, Stout moved to Chicago, and died in 1927 as one of Chicago's 10 wealthiest men, having also been railroad and electric company president and owning timber in the South and West.

In 1911, after a few other owners, the Archdiocese of Dubuque bought it as its office headquarters and home for the Archbishop, and operated it as such for nearly 75 years.

Today, guests check in at the reception hall, paneled in rosewood. The library is open for guest's use, where they can read by a green onyx fireplace. Rolltop bookcases are built in to the walls, and onyx and mosaics are used in several places.

Like the Redstone Inn, the house has been furnished with period furniture, all obtained within 100 miles of Dubuque. Some original furnishings remain, like the grandfather clock in the reception hall and the stained glass windows. Unlike the Redstone Inn, this building was kept almost in original condition by its previous owners. A second-floor lounge has a color TV and phone for guests' use.

Rooms: Five - #21 has double bed with Italian marble bath. #22 and #23 have queens, share Italian marble bath - $55; #25 and #26 have queens, share a bath - $45. Rooms are done in antiques and brass beds. Baths have a tub and shower; third person over 12 - $10. Cribs $5. Add tax.

Meals: Continental breakfast included, served in the dining room, which features an inlaid mosaic fireplace hearth.

Dates open: Year 'round   **Smoking:** Yes

Children: Yes (cribs available)   **Pets:** No

Nearby: Fourth Street Elevator (189-foot cable car), Five Flags civic center/theater, historic preservation districts with shops, historic museum, riverboat rides, greyhound racing, walking tours.

Directions from Twin Cities: Check maps; either follow the Mississippi or go south on I-35 and then east. Inn is easy to find in downtown Dubuque.

Deposit: First night's lodging or confirmation by credit card

Payment: Cash, personal or traveler's checks, VISA, MasterCard or AMEX

The DeSoto House Hotel
230 S. Main   Owners:
Galena, IL   Mortgage Consultants/Investment Properties
815-777-0090   General Manager: Cary Turecamo

When the DeSoto House was re-opened in April 1986 after a massive $8 million renovation, a headline in the local paper noted, "History marches through the DeSoto House." That's close to literal truth. Parades and 25,000 people gathered to welcome home Galena resident Gen. Ulysses S. Grant from the Civil War in 1865. Abraham Lincoln spoke against slavery from the DeSoto balcony in 1856, and Stephen Douglas spoke there two years later. Over the years, nine presidents visited, including Teddy Roosevelt. History more likely tiptoed through the DeSoto House when it hosted Mark Twain, Susan B. Anthony, Horace Greely and Ralph Waldo Emerson.

Opened in prosperous Galena in 1855, the $85,000 hotel was heralded as "the best hotel west of New York City." Indeed, Chicago was then rivaled by Galena, with her bulging lead mines and busy river traffic, and the five-story hotel was the epitome of elegance in that era. The hotel survived a 1859 fire and the 1880 removal of her two top stories, but barely weathered the years when economic depression gripped Galena. Structurally unsound and posted as dangerous in 1978, the hotel stood empty for the first time while city officials and developers began feasibility studies and funding searches.

Finally, after a year of restoration and new construction, the hotel re-opened with two restaurants and a bakery, a parking ramp, five meeting and banquet rooms, cocktail lounges and a ballroom. Shops and meeting rooms are on the street level, facing an open court yard. Woodwork and masonry has been preserved wherever possible. All hotel amenities, including room service, valet parking and bell boys, are present.

Rooms: 55 - Each with private bath, writing table, color cable TV and phone, decorated individually in period reproductions with country wallpapers. About half have a view of the Galena River and Grant's Park. Four rooms have handicapped access. Singles, $65-85; $100 and $180 for suites. Doubles, $75-95; $110 and $190 for suites. Add tax.

Meals: Three meals a day available in hotel dining rooms and bakery.

Dates open: Year 'round   **Smoking:** Yes

Children: Yes (under 10 free)   **Pets:** No

Nearby: Galena's streets are like an 1880s movie set with fine architecture and historic walking tours. Museum, 1 block. Antique shops, restaurants, gift shops next door and down the street. Park, 1 block.

Directions from Twin Cities: Pull out the map. From Highway 61 to LaCrosse, there are a couple options for a beautiful drive. Hotel is on right side of Main Street, about one block from floodgates.

Deposit: First night's lodging

Payment: Cash, personal or traveler's checks, VISA, MasterCard, AMEX, or Diners Club

The Farmers' Home Hotel B&B

334 Spring St.
Galena, IL 61036
815-777-3456

Owners/Operators:
Tom Kristianson and Floyd Mansberger
Innkeeper: Rachel Stilson

In the 1860s, when farmers came to market in Galena, they often could not make a return wagon trip in one day. The 10-room Farmers' Home Hotel, two blocks from downtown, "was a little step higher than a boarding house," said Tom Kristianson. Rooms were located over a store and bakery, built and run by the Vogel brothers, a busy place in Galena's heyday.

The Galena Gazette once reported that for nearly a century the Vogel name meant "honesty and fair deals," and one gets the sense that Kristianson and Mansberger, the first owners outside the Vogel family, intend to carry on the tradition. Their restoration work has made the hotel modern while maintaining or authentically restoring as much as possible, including the original room numbers on doors and "fake graining" in woodwork. "We're real purists," Kristianson said. "We don't equate bad restoration with bad taste, we equate it with immorality."

When the two friends bought the hotel in January 1985, only a few downstairs rooms were being used. They acted as general contractors, used plenty of their own sweat equity, and saw that the floor plan stayed the same. The building needed to be re-wired, re-plumbed, re-plastered, re-ceilinged, wallpapered, carpeted, air conditioned and wired for cable TV, which is available by request. Seven rooms opened in May 1986.

Downstairs, the former store and bakery are a meeting room and a breakfast restaurant, open to the public. Anything off the menu is included in guests' room rates (tips not included). Don't be surprised if Mansberger, an archeologist, cooks up his Hobo Hash himself.

Rooms: Seven - All with private baths with tubs and phones. Antique brass and wood double beds. Decorated with antiques, comforters and quilts, and country wallpaper, in beiges, light purples and whites. Doubles are $65; off-season discounts. Add tax.

Meals: Breakfast downstairs in restaurant, included in room rate. Menu includes award-winning local bacon, Floyd's Hobo Hash (potatoes, onions, bacon or ham, broccoli and cheese, covered with cheddar and sour cream), omelettes, eggs, fruit pancakes and fresh squeezed orange juice.

Dates open: Year 'round   **Smoking:** Not in rooms

Children: Over 10   **Pets:** No

Nearby: Downtown Galena, with historic walking tours, shops and restaurants, 2 blocks.

Directions from Twin Cities: Highway 61 south to LaCrosse; two routes to choose from through Wisconsin down to the southwest corner. Galena is 20 miles south of Dubuque, Iowa.

Deposit: First night's lodging

Payment: Cash, personal or traveler's checks, VISA or MasterCard

Guest Houses in Galena, Illinois

The Galena/Jo Daviess County Chamber of Commerce
Convention & Visitors Bureau
101 Bouthillier St.
Galena, IL 61036
815-777-0203
Outside Illinois: 1-800-874-9377

Galena, an historic little town about 20 miles from Dubuque, has the Midwest's highest concentration of B&Bs and guest houses. The county was up to 30 last time a count was taken. Many of the houses date back to the 1800s, such as the 1838 brick home Pat Laury runs as Mother's Country Inn.

The Convention & Visitors Bureau provides a great service: call them toll-free and they will tell you which homes still have openings for the night you desire. That saves you a lot of calling the homes directly. Write for a brochure, "Eat, Sleep and Camp in Galena," for information on lodging. Those listed below are in Galena; others are in nearby Stockton, some are on farms. Add tax.

Aldrich Guest House, 900 Third St.; 815-777-3323; Judy Green. Four rooms, full breakfast, children over 8 welcome; $45-55.

Bell-Aire Mansion, Highway 20 W; 815-777-0893; Evelyn or Jim Nemecek. Four rooms, children welcome; $40-45.

Colonial Guest House, 1004 Park Ave.; 815-777-0336; Mary Keller. Five rooms, continental breakfast, children welcome, one room handicapped accessible, two with kitchens; $35-40.

Comfort Guest House, 1000 Third St.; 815-777-3062; Connie or Tom Sola. Three rooms, full breakfast, children 14 and older welcome; $35.

Farster's Executive Suites, 815-777-9125, Robert Farstar. Two suites located above a downtown storefront just recently opened.

Felt Manor Guest House, 125 S. Prospect St.; 815-777-9093; Sandy or Terry Hemlock. Four rooms, full breakfast, children over 12 welcome, huge mansion on hill above town; $45-55.

Fricke Guest House, 119 S. Bench St.; 815-777-1193/9430; Virginia or William Hunt. Two rooms, full breakfast, children welcome; two parlors, a pump organ and grand piano, $40-45.

Gallery Guest Suite, 204.5 S. Main St.; 815-777-1510; Marilyn or Carl Johnson, Jr. One three-room apartment overlooking Main Street, one double-bed, not suitable for young children; $40; $200/week.

The Lafayette Guest House, 911 Third St.; 815-777-1160; Shirley Hulscher. Four rooms, kitchen available, children welcome; $45.

Log Cabin Guest House, 11661 W. Chetlain Lane; 815-777-2845; Linda or Scott Ettleman. Two rooms, children welcome, kitchen available, coffee provided; $30-40.

Mother's Country Inn, 349 Spring St.; 815-777-3153; Patricia Laury. Seven rooms, continental breakfast, children welcome; $35-45.

Pillsbury Guest House, 713 S. Bench St.; 815-777-1611; Irma or Guy Pillsbury. Three rooms, continental breakfast, children 12 and over welcome, sauna and exercise equipment; $50-60.

Spring Street Guest House, 418 Spring St.; 815-777-0354; Sandra or Charles Fach. One suite with king-sized bed, full breakfast, older children welcome, $59.95.

Stillman Manor Inn, 513 Bouthillier St.; 815-777-0557; Julianne or Marilyn Jensen. Seven rooms, some with fireplaces, full breakfast during week, children welcome; $33.50-48.50.

Victorian Mansion, 301 S. High St.; 815-777-0675; more than six rooms furnished in authentic Victorian antiques; children discouraged; $45-60.

Cooper Hill House

33 S. Sixth St.
P.O. Box 5
Bayfield, WI 54814
715-779-5060

Owners/Operators:
Sheree and Phil Peterson

"I'd always gone by this house and thought, 'Geez, what you could do with a house like this,' " said Phil Peterson. What you could do, he and Sheree, his wife, and a partner found out, is reroof, insulate, replumb, change doorways, add bathrooms, and paint the place yellow.

But now that that's done, the Petersons (who have since bought out their partner) get to live in the 1888 home and meet lots of nice visitors who want to stay there, too. The home is about eight blocks from Lake Superior on Cooper Hill, named after a local family. The hill was a favorite for bobsledding in the early 1900s.

For materials, the original builders, Mary and Martin Johnson, used hemlock and white pine from Henry Wachsmuth's lumberyard. Johnson was a millwright there, but later his employer would own the home, purchasing it as a wedding gift for his son. Wachsmuth was a young entrepreneur, having opened his lumber company at age 25. His descendents owned the home until Petersons bought it with Rick Thompson in the fall of 1983. The B&B opened in June 1984.

Phil Peterson came to Bayfield in 1977 as a manager for a sailboat charter; Sheree came in 1978 as a park service employee. All furnishings in their B&B are antiques; the dining room buffet came from a home on one of the Apostle Islands. The bathroom sinks were purchased from the Curtis Hotel in Minneapolis before it was demolished - look underneath to see where Phil has written the room number from which the sink came. Guests may use the living and dining rooms, the large porch and the yard, with lawn chairs.

Rooms and Rates: Four - All with private baths, done in antiques with Curtis Hotel sinks. Rose Room - queen bed, shower - $49; Brass Room - double bed, shower - $49; Green Room - white iron double bed, shower and tub - $44; Bittersweet Room, dark iron double bed, view of Long Island light at night, shower - $44. $3 less for singles; add tax. Discounts in non-peak seasons.

Meals: Breakfast is continental, served in the dining room 8 - 9:45 a.m. and includes fresh fruit; juice, coffee, teas; homemade muffins or breads; homemade jams.

Dates open: May - October; winter by reservation   **Pets:** No

Smoking: On front porch only   **Children:** "At parents' discretion"

Nearby: In Bayfield historic district; headquarters to Apostle Islands National Lakeshore, 3 blocks; ferry to Madeline Island, excursion boats, marina, shops, restaurants, 5-8 blocks.

Directions from Twin Cities: I-35 to Taylors Falls/Highway 8 or Grantsburg/Highway 70 east to 63 at either Shell Lake or Spooner; or I-35 to Duluth; north/east to U.S. 2 east to Highway 13 at eastern city limits of Ashland; north on Highway 13 for 19 miles; Highway 13 turns into Sixth St., house is on the left.

Deposit: Half of room rate

Payment: Cash, personal or traveler's checks, VISA or MasterCard

Greunke's Inn

17 Rittenhouse Ave.
P.O. Box 768
Bayfield, WI 54814
715-779-5480

Owners/Operators:
Judith Lokken-Strom and Alan Waite

Nazar LaBonte was a French-Canadian who ended up in Bayfield, but not by choice. Having lost his money while gambling on board a ferry from Detroit to Superior, Wis., the crew off-loaded him in LaPointe on Madeline Island in the early 1860s.

Making the best of a bad situation, LaBonte went to work logging off the Bayfield peninsula, and soon opened the "LaBonte House," explains Alan Waite. The boarding house was downtown in Bayfield's busiest intersection and operated until the 1920s.

Eventually modernized and converted to a restaurant downstairs, the place achieved its most pleasing reputation under the ownership of Vic and Irene Greunke, who bought it in the 1940s and ran a restaurant and inn until 1975. Greunke's Inn was the local gathering spot, and rooms upstairs often went to fishermen and hunters.

Judith and Alan now run the inn and restaurant. In 1983, they did some remodeling, including adding bathrooms to some rooms. Putting in new fiberboard ceilings and baths, wallpapering and furnishing with antiques acquired through the years, they have maintained one of the oldest continuously operating business in Bayfield. The layout of the upstairs guest rooms remains essentially the same as in Nazar LaBonte's day.

Rooms and Rates: Seven, and one two-bedroom apartment - Two showers and a half-bath in the hall; some rooms with half-baths. All can use porch with lake view. Examples include #1 with blonde birdseye maple antique double and twin beds, done in yellows, shares bath; #3 has an antique wooden queen with half-bath, done in tan and rose; the apartment has one bedroom, a loft, a bathroom with shower, TV and kitchen. $30 - $50, depending on season. Add tax.

Meals: Full breakfast menu available in the restaurant downstairs, which is open 6 a.m. - 10 p.m. daily.

Dates open: Mid-April through mid-October

Smoking and Pets: "Not encouraged"   **Children:** Yes (under 6 free)

Nearby: In Bayfield historic district; headquarters to Apostle Islands National Lakeshore, 5 blocks. Madeline Island ferry dock, shops, restaurants, excursion boats, city park/beach, 1-2 blocks.

Directions from Twin Cities: I-35 to Taylors Falls/Highway 8 or Grantsburg/Highway 70 east to 63 at either Shell Lake or Spooner; or I-35 to Duluth; north/east to U.S. 2 east to Highway 13 at eastern city limits of Ashland; north on Highway 13 for 19 miles to Bayfield. Follow 13 through town; Greunke's on left at main intersection downtown.

Deposit: Half of room rate

Payment: Cash, personal or traveler's checks, VISA or MasterCard

Grey Oak Guest House

Seventh and Manypenny
P.O. Box 584
Bayfield, WI 54814
715-779-5111

Operator:
    Old Rittenhouse Inn
Innkeepers:
    Susan Larsen and Neil Howk

Ervin Leighy was one businessman who had a vision for Bayfield's future, a future that the town would survive past the lumbering, brownstone quarrying and fishing era of the late 1800s and early 1900s. And he put his money where his mouth was: his residence had a full brownstone foundation, guaranteed to last practically forever.

The 1888 home was built on what was then the outskirts of town. Now, the house is within the Bayfield Historic District and what might be considered the middle of town, though Bayfield has only 800 residents.

The home stayed in the Leighy family until the 30s, when it was acquired by the Hadland family. Eventually, an apartment was constructed on the second floor, but the home remained otherwise structurally unchanged.

When the Hadland family wanted to sell, Susan Larsen was interested. She and her husband had come to Bayfield as National Park Service employees. Susan since began work for Mary and Jerry Phillips at the Old Rittenhouse Inn. A partnership was formed to buy, redo and rent the house, the third property run by the Old Rittenhouse Inn.

While some of the original floors remain, major renovation was necessary. Walls were rebuilt to make three large guest rooms, new plumbing was added, the house was insulated and rewired, and fireplaces were added. Guests have use of the living room with fireplace and front porch.

Rooms and Rates: Three - All with private bath with tubs and showers, queen sized brass beds and fireplaces. Upstairs is a two-room suite with a sofa bed, done in mauve and green - $88. Downstairs are two rooms, one in cranberry with hardwood floors, and the other in grey and mauve, both $78. Add tax.

Meals: Continental breakfast included, by reservation at the Old Rittenhouse Inn, 4 blocks away. Full breakfast available.

Dates open: May - October; some weekends rest of winter

Smoking: Yes   **Pets:** No   **Children:** Yes

Nearby: In Bayfield historic district; headquarters to Apostle Islands National Lakeshore, 5 blocks; excursion boats and ferry to Madeline Island, marina, restaurants, shops, 7-9 blocks.

Directions from Twin Cities: I-35 to Taylors Falls/Highway 8 or Grantsburg/Highway 70 east to 63 at either Shell Lake or Spooner; or I-35 to Duluth; north/east to U.S. 2 east to Highway 13 at eastern city limits of Ashland; north on Highway 13 for 19 miles. Turn left on either 7th or Manypenny to corner.

Deposit: First night's lodging

Payment: Cash, personal or traveler's checks, VISA or MasterCard

Le Chateau Boutin

7 Rice Street
P.O. Box 584
Bayfield, WI 54814
715-779-5111

Owners/Operators:
Mary and Jerry Phillips,
Greg Carrier

This National Register of Historic Places home was built in 1907 for lumber baron Frank Boutin, Jr., who used it as a year 'round family home. Boutin was a busy Bayfield businessman, also starting a fishing fleet. Despite touches like detailed stained and leaded glass, Boutin's wife didn't like life in Bayfield, and they moved to California after five years in the home.

The Elmore family of Chicago then used the place as a summer home, adding formal gardens, but it was lost in the stock market crash.

Early on, a clause put into the sales agreement stated ownership would revert to the local Catholic church should the home be foreclosed upon. The church assumed ownership several times over the next decades, finally using it as a convent for nuns who taught at the local school.

Paul Turner bought it from the church in the '70s, providing a bit more local color and excitement than the good sisters had. Turner renamed it The Mansion, rented rooms and gave tours, which sometimes included his playing a massive organ from the third floor ballroom.

In failing health, Turner sold to the new owners. They opened the B&B in July 1985 after extensive renovation. The original seven-leaf mahogany Chippendale dining room table, imported from Paris, remains from Boutin's era, as does the stained and leaded glass. Guests have use of the living and music rooms and the huge porch, and get a tour of the home.

Rooms and Rates: Six - All with private bath, five with fireplaces. Examples include the North East Room, with a double door to porch, an original black walnut bed with angels carved to guard sleepers, fireplace - $88; the Tower Room is done in tiger birch, double bed, $68. Turret Suite is former men's poker room plus women's game room, with seven windows and sitting room, king brass bed - $98. Third floor South Room in blue and white has sloping ceilings, queen bed - $78. Add tax.

Meals: Continental breakfast included, served by reservation at the Old Rittenhouse Inn, 4 blocks away. Full breakfast available.

Dates open: May - October; some weekends rest of winter

Smoking: Yes   **Pets:** No   **Children:** Yes

Nearby: In Bayfield historic district; headquarters to Apostle Islands National Lakeshore, 4 blocks; excursion boats and ferry to Madeline Island, marina, restaurants, shops, 3-6 blocks.

Directions from Twin Cities: I-35 to Taylors Falls/Highway 8 or Grantsburg/Highway 70 east to 63 at either Shell Lake or Spooner; or I-35 to Duluth; north/east to U.S. 2 east to Highway 13 at eastern city limits of Ashland; north on Highway 13 for 19 miles. Follow 13 almost out of town, turn left on Rice.

Deposit: First night's lodging

Payment: Cash, personal or traveler's checks, VISA or MasterCard

Old Rittenhouse Inn

Rittenhouse and Third
P.O. Box 584
Bayfield, WI 54814
715-779-5111

Owners/Operators:
Mary and Jerry Phillips

When Mary and Jerry Phillips opened a B&B in a Bayfield mansion in the summer of 1974, they didn't know that's what they were doing. The concept hadn't reached the Midwest yet. "The place had been used as a boarding house at one time, and we were getting calls since there was a shortage of rooms in town," Jerry said. "We said, 'Maybe we should take a couple rooms a night.' " Food lovers that they are, they soon added gourmet breakfasts.

Today, the Old Rittenhouse Inn is a nine-room country inn, expanded once, with elegant dining on the first floor. The Phillips also operate two other Bayfield B&Bs.

While teaching music in Madison, the couple bought the 26-room 1890 summer home of Civil War Gen. Allen Fuller, going against the advice of friends and relatives. "They thought we were nuts," Jerry said. "We simply bought it because we fell in love with the house. It was 1973, kerosene was 18 cents a gallon, and we thought we'd come up a couple times in the winter."

Restoration and filling the inn with antiques, plus the energy crisis and a few other factors, led to the need for a decision to be or not to be full-time innkeepers. After a sabbatical and visiting country inns in the East, they opted for Bayfield. Eventually lunches and dinners were added, and meals became more elaborate; Mary is still chef. Five guest rooms were added in 1984. A mail-order business has been started to offer preserves and other treats.

Rooms and Rates: Nine - All with private bath and antiques or reproductions; eight have working fireplaces; $58, $78 or $88, plus $15 for additional person. Examples include Room 1, with original antique bed from the Fuller home and a lakeview - $58; Room 3 has lake view, original sink bowl and shower only - $78; Room 4 has a king bed with headboard goes to the ceiling - $88; Room 6 has white iron and brass bed, balcony- $88. Two rooms on first floor have wheelchair access. Add tax.

Meals: Continental breakfast included by reservation: fresh fruit, juice, homemade breads with homemade preserves, coffee or tea. Full breakfast available; open for breakfast for guests only, with exception of Sunday brunch. Lunch and dinner available; reservations requested.

Dates open: May - October; weekends rest of winter; closed January

Smoking: Yes   **Children:** Yes   **Pets:** No

Nearby: In Bayfield historic district; headquarters to Apostle Islands National Lakeshore, excursion boats and ferry to Madeline Island, restaurants, marina, 2 blocks.

Directions from Twin Cities: I-35 to Taylors Falls/Highway 8 or Grantsburg/Highway 70 east to 63 at either Shell Lake or Spooner; or I-35 to Duluth; north/east on U.S. 2 to Highway 13 at eastern city limits of Ashland; north on Highway 13 for 19 miles. Highway 13 turns into Rittenhouse Ave.

Deposit: First night's lodging

Payment: Cash, personal or traveler's checks, VISA or MasterCard

Pinehurst Inn

Rt. 1, Box 222
Bayfield, WI 54314
715-779-3676

Owner/Operator:
Michele and Keith Ochsner

Despite six months of work before the family opened their B&B, not all family members were playing on the same team. No sooner had Keith Ochsner hung out the Pinehurst Inn shingle with the help of two young sons and returned to the basement when the first customers pulled in. The boys glared at them and one warned, "You get out of here." They did.

After a fatherly chat, the tables turned. It was the busy July 4th weekend, 1983, and "we were full in 20 minutes with the woodwork still tacky from the turpentine and linseed oil."

The 1895 structure looked much different six months before, after years of disuse, when Ochsners became the third owners. Floors were leveled, walls replastered, ceilings redone, bathrooms added and rewiring and redecorating finished.

This is the home's second round of innhood. The second owner offered meals at the house for people staying in cabins on the beach across the highway. "There was an extra charge for electricity and guests had to provide references," Keith said. That ended abruptly during a freak flood in 1942, when 8.52 inches of rain in 12 hours caused the nearby creek to wash the beach cabins out into Lake Superior. There was a daring night-time rescue in which people in the cabins crawled up to the roof tops to be saved.

The first owner, who never rented rooms, was R.D. Pike. Wealthy sawmill owner Pike had the home designed by William Price, a Philadelphia architect. Only about 15 of his buildings are still standing; this one is on the National Register of Historic Places. Guests may use the living room with fireplace, library and dining room, porch, lawn, picnic tables and garden.

Rooms and Rates: Four - Room 1 has lake view, two queen beds, done in greens and browns with mallards on the wallpaper, private bath with clawfoot tub and sitting room - $65. Room 2 has king bed, done in blue with x-c skiiers, clawfoot tub and private bath - $50. Room 3 has queen bed, done in blue with seashell motif - $45. Room 4 has a double brass bed, light blues - $40. Rooms 3 and 4 share bath with tub and shower. Add tax.

Meals: Breakfast is served family-style in the dining room at 8:30 and may include fresh fruit in season; juice, coffee, tea; waffles, French Toast, pancakes, quiche or scrambled eggs.

Dates open: Year 'round   **Smoking:** "Ambivalent"

Children: Yes   **Pets:** Yes

Nearby: DNR fish hatchery, next door; walk to Lake Superior, across highway; ski hill and groomed x-c ski trails; ferry dock and Bayfield shops, restaurants, etc., 2.5 miles.

Directions from Twin Cities: I-35 to Taylors Falls/Highway 8 or Grantsburg/Highway 70 east to 63 at either Shell Lake or Spooner; north to U.S. 2 east to Highway 13 at eastern city limits of Ashland; north on Highway 13 about 17 miles. Pinehurst Inn is on the left.

Deposit: First night's lodging

Payment: Cash, personal or traveler's checks, VISA or MasterCard

Woods Manor B&B

P.O. Box 196
LaPointe, WI 54850
715-747-3102

Owners/Operators:
Woody and Gail Peterson

This Madeline Island B&B is still in the family of the original owner. Woody Peterson is the great grandson of the builder, F.H. Woods, a Lincoln, Nebraska, man. Woods first came to Madeline Island with his father in the late 1800s, looking for relief from asthma or hay fever.

Woods became acquainted with a Missourian, Hunter Gary, and the two went into business together after hearing about a new telephone device invented by an angry mortician. The mortician, Peterson explains, was angry at telephone operators. When the mortician's best friend died, the operator had switched the call for the business of embalming and burying the friend to a competitor. So, to eradicate powerful operators, the mortician devised the telephone dial. "He just wanted revenge," Peterson says, so he allowed Woods and Gary to patent the device, which they did, and very successfully at that. The two became neighbors on Madeline Island.

Woods built Woods Manor in the early 1920s with huge timber ceiling beams and plaster walls with oval window frames, resembling Mediterranean decor. He had a 140-foot yacht with which he toured the Apostle Islands. Both Coolidge and Pershing were acquaintances and they visited.

Peterson opened the manor as a B&B in July 1985. Guests have use of the huge living room with a grand piano from the 1920s, porch and dining room with fireplaces in each, stereo system, satellite TV and swimming. The grounds stretch to the lake and a clay tennis court is in back. An outdoor hot tub bubbles off the living room, bikes are free for guests' use, and Peterson plans on installing a sauna and dock.

Rooms and Rates: Seven - Two rooms have king-sized brass beds, one has a queen, two have antique provincial twin beds, one has a small double, and a king and queen downstairs share a bath and are a suite. Two baths have showers only. $50 May 1-22 and Oct. 6-27; $65 May 23-June 27 and Sept. 1-Oct. 5; $75 June 28-Aug. 31. Add tax.

Meals: Breakfast is from 7:30 - 10 in the dining room and is continental, including rolls, fresh fruit, coffee cakes, cold cereals, juices, tea and coffee.

Dates open: May 1 - Oct. 31   **Children:** Yes

Smoking: Yes (owner does)   **Pets:** Check with owner

Nearby: Ferry dock, shops, restaurants, museum, municipal tennis courts in LaPointe, 3 blocks; golf course with rental clubs, 3/4 mile; swimming, sailing, windsurfing, hiking, biking, camping, beachcombing on island.

Directions from Twin Cities: I-35 to Taylors Falls/Highway 8 or Grantsburg/Highway 70 east to 63 at either Shell Lake or Spooner; or I-35 to Duluth; north/east to U.S. 2 east to Highway 13 at eastern city limits of Ashland; north on Highway 13 for 19 miles to Bayfield; follow 13 to ferry dock. Off ferry, turn left and follow road along homes to Woods Manor.

Deposit: Half of room rate

Payment: Cash, personal or traveler's checks, VISA, MasterCard or AMEX

The Kettle Falls Hotel

Voyageurs National Park
P.O. Box 50
International Falls, MN 56649
218-283-9821

Owner:
  National Park Service
Operator:
  Chuck Williams

This historic hotel, accessible only by water, is undergoing a $2.1 million rehabilitation and probably will reopen the spring of 1988.

Listed on the National Register of Historic Places, the hotel was built in 1913 near the American Channel where Rainy Lake empties into Namakan Lake (to find it on a map of Voyageurs National Park, it is on a northeastern part of the park where, if one looks south, one will look into Canada).

A man named Ed Rose built the hotel to rent rooms to construction workers building the Kettle Falls Dam. It was one of two dams constructed on Namakan Lake; logging company president Edward Backus wanted a series of dams to control the lake's water levels and boost his sawmills' production, but Canadian and American legislators would agree to only two.

Logging was big business in the area for years (before that, gold miners portaged around Kettle Falls to get to Little American Island, where gold was discovered in 1893; and before that, Indians and voyageurs used the portage in their fur trading treks). Loggers also would account for some of Rose's business at the 20-room hotel.

The docks that Rose had built to serve the hotel figured prominately in the fishing industry, as well. During the 1920s, fish buyers would gather there weekly to meet the commerical fishing fleet. The National Park Service quotes one area resident recalling the selling: "When the fish boats used to come in, buyers would bid for fish just like they used to for cotton...Fish sold for 2.5 to 5 cents a pound."

Up to 5,000 100-pound fish boxes a year were shipped via rail to Chicago and other cities. When a road opened in 1920 near Orr, Minn., use of the docks began to decline.

By 1918, however, Robert Williams ("Grandpa Bob" to concessionaire Chuck Williams) had bought the hotel for $1,000 and four barrels of whiskey. Whiskey was sold for 25 cents and a beer would cost a dime with lunch.

During Prohibition, stills were hidden in the woods and illegal booze was sold in shacks near the hotel. (Good booze was said to bring $300 a case.) And, as the Park Service delicately puts it, "as in any frontier settlement, the oldest profession flourished."

Times are no longer so wild at the hotel, which has three housekeeping cabins for rent until the hotel re-opens.

But much of the original hotel will remain, including the rolling floor of the bar, caused by dirt from the hill behind the hotel washing underneath. While there will be 12 rooms upstairs, instead of 20, the two communal baths with original sinks will remain. Bar and dining service again will be offered guests (dinner will be open to the public). A screened porch will be replaced, and $2 million worth of new rental units will be added.

Visitors may get to the hotel by floatplane, their own boat, rented boat or boat service offered by Williams or area resorts. The route is from Ash River Trail over 17 miles of water. The Park Service now offers naturalist-guided trips to the Kettle Falls Historic District, which are expected to continue.

21 Questions

Who says history isn't interesting? Test yourself by naming the correct historic hotel, B&B or country inn. Answers are on page 127.

1. Soo Line put up property and money to build which hotel?

2. When A.A. Cooper built his daughter a mansion for a wedding gift, he built a 27-room duplex so it could generate income if her husband could not. Name this inn.

3. The "Miss Woods Girls" -- young women enrolled in the Miss Woods School for teacher training -- once used this home as a dorm.

4. What hotel hired, and reportedly fired, Sinclair Lewis?

5. "Ma" Pennington made which inn famous by serving chicken dinners using the chickens raised out in back?

6. Where can guests catch trout in a private stocked stream the same way the wealthy founder of this estate once did?

7. Name the B&B that is the former estate of one of the men who patented the telephone dial.

8. In which two facilities can you find furnishings from the no-longer-standing Curtis Hotel of Minneapolis?

9. This home once rented beach cabins until a freak flood washed them out into Lake Superior, prompting a daring night-time rescue to pluck guests from the cabin roof tops.

10. Once a brewery, which facility survived Prohibition by selling soda pop, "near beer" and cigars?

11. In the 1970s, rooms here rented for $2.50 to $12.50 a night, and truckers often took showers for $1 in what is now the sitting room.

12. What former boarding house was built by a French-Canadian who was thrown off a ferry after losing his money gambling?

13. Name the hotel that, since it opened in 1877, has traded hands 31 times.

14. Which hotel admits to once breaking occupancy records of sorts by renting one room 10 times in one night?

15. Babe Ruth and Jack Dempsey were once members of this private club, which goes by the same name today.

16. Though the sill and sash manufacturer who owned this home also owned a whole block of town, he lost this home for back taxes.

17. Which hotel rated a special stop on passenger trains so passengers could eat a meal at "Clara's"?

18. Name the facility which reverted to the ownership of the local Catholic church every time it was foreclosed upon, and served as a convent for nuns teaching at the local school.

19. From the balcony of which hotel did Abraham Lincoln speak against slavery?

20. Which inn was a former combination furniture store/mortuary with three owners, the Thompson and Thompson brothers, the Thompson and Thompson brothers, and the Johnsons?

21. Name the B&B which is making history today as the only B&B in an innovative "ski-through" program, where guests cross-country ski between lodging establishments and their luggage is waiting for them.

Contents Grouped By Category*

Country Inns: Page:

Historic Hotels:

Please note that these categories were assigned by the author, who is fully aware that someone, somewhere is going to strongly disagree. Some of the decisions are arguable; please read the full descriptions and the definitions in the introduction, then decide for yourself.

**Assume Minnesota unless state is indicated*

Contents Grouped By Location

Travel Notes

Travel Notes

Travel Notes

21 Answers

to the Quiz on pages 118-119:

1. Thayer Hotel, Annandale
2. The Redstone Inn, Dubuque
3. Evelo's B&B, Minneapolis
4. Palmer House Hotel, Sauk Centre
5. Afton House Inn, Afton
6. Seven Pines Lodge, Lewis, WI
7. Woods Manor, LaPointe (Madeline Island), WI
8. Cooper Hill House, Bayfield, WI , and the American House, Morris
9. Pinehurst Inn, Bayfield
10. Fitger's Inn, Duluth
11. Schumacher's New Prague Hotel, New Prague
12. Greunke's Inn, Bayfield
13. The Archer House, Northfield
14. The Hotel, Winona
15. The Naniboujou Lodge, North Shore North of Grand Marais
16. Carriage House B&B, Winona
17. The St. James Hotel, Red Wing
18. Le Chateau Boutin, Bayfield
19. The DeSoto House Hotel, Galena, IL
20. Mrs. B's Historic Lanesboro Inn, Lanesboro
21. Young's Island B&B, Gunflint Trail/Grand Marais

Copies of **Room at the Inn** make a great gift for all travelers: couples, singles or families, vacationers or businesspeople.

Room at the Inn is also a must-have for people planning a
 Δ wedding
 Δ family reunion
 Δ anniversary celebration
 Δ business or group meeting, retreat or trip.
Businesses will find the guide useful for employees who travel and when hosting consultants, speakers or new employees.

Additional copies may be ordered from **Down to Earth Publications, 873 Lincoln, St. Paul, MN 55105** at $9.20 each, including postage and handling (Minnesota Residents add 6% sales tax, please - 55 cents - for a total of $9.75). Make checks payable to Down to Earth Publications.

- -

Order Form

Mail to: **Down to Earth Publications**
    873 Lincoln
    St. Paul, MN 55105

Cost is $9.20 (includes postage and handling).
Minnesota Residents: Please add 6% sales tax (55 cents) - total $9.75.

I have enclosed $_____ for _____ book(s). Send it/them to:

Name: _____

Street: _____ Apt. No. _____

City: _____ State: _____ Zip: _____